With Grant *at* Fort Donelson, Shiloh *and* Vicksburg

And an Appreciation of General U. S. Grant

By

WILBUR F. CRUMMER

of the 45th Regt., Ill. Vols.

With Illustrations

Published 1915

By E. C. CRUMMER & CO.

Oak Park, Ill.

Marula

An imprint of Arcadia Publishing

With Grant at Fort Donelson, Shiloh and Vicksburg
and an Appreciation of General U.S. Grant
by Wilbur Fisk Crummer

A Marula Historical Reprint
Originally published in 1915

Published by Arcadia Publishing
Charleston SC

ISBN 978-0-7385-9494-1

Printed in the United States of America

For all general information contact Arcadia Publishing at:
Telephone 843-853-2070
Fax 843-853-0044
E-mail sales@arcadiapublishing.com
For customer service and orders:
Toll-Free 1-888-313-2665

Visit us on the Internet at www.arcadiapublishing.com

Yours truly
Wilbur F. Crummer

Table of Contents

Illustrations

FOREWORD

In this year of 1915, when the sounds of battle and strife come wafted to us across the sea from Europe, the younger generation are asking questions of the Veterans of the Civil War about their experiences in battle.

Formerly I lived in Galena, Ill., and having been personally acquainted with, and a neighbor of General U. S. Grant, and one of the "Boys in Blue" who followed him in the battles of Fort Donelson, Shiloh and Vicksburg, I deem it my privilege to add my mite to the history that clusters round the greatest military genius of modern times.

To please many friends who have heard my lectures on the Civil War, and at the request of my children, the following pages have been written, from data made at the time and since, and from a vivid memory of the stirring days of 1862 and 1863.

WILBUR F. CRUMMER.

Oak Park, Ill., June 14, 1915.

FORT HENRY

CHAPTER I.

"Say, Will, did you see that one as it crossed the line just now?"

"No, Jim; how can a feller see anything this dark night?"

"Well, he ran right by me, and I think he was as big as our dog, Rover, at home. Isn't it a beastly shame that orders are so strict about shooting while on guard? I'd like to have shot that fellow for sure."

"Never mind, Jim; you'll have enough of shooting before this war is over, I'm thinking, for I feel it in my bones that Gen. Grant is getting ready to start something in the way of fighting, for I've seen him two or three times, and he looks to me as though he was a fighter."

"Well, old scout, anything but this kind of soldiering."

The conversation was between two young

soldier boys of Company A, 45th Illinois Volunteers, while on guard duty around camp in the month of January, 1862, at Cairo, Illinois, on one of the darkest and rainiest nights they ever saw. The "It" was a calf that in crossing the path had startled Jim so much he was tempted to shoot it. As the two neighbor boys, just from the farm in Northern Illinois, trudged back and forth on their posts through the deepest and blackest mud they had ever seen, they stopped at the end of their "beat" as they met, and talked for a few moments of home and the loved ones left behind; of camp and its arduous duties, of drilling and guard duty, and then of what would be the next move. The American Volunteers always kept up a "think" or two in their heads as to what would and should be done in fighting the battles for the Union.

"Will, I hope we won't have to stay here long."

"You bet we won't," responds Will. "Grant

has got something up his sleeve and we'll be moving before long, take my word for it."

Will was right. In a few days a large number of steamboats gathered at the wharf, and were being loaded with ammunition, commissary stores and all the needed accessories of an army, and then the day came to break camp and the boys marched on the boats, wondering which way the boats would head out in the river.

On February 4th, 1862, the boats are loaded to the guards and the order is given, and with Gen. Grant leading the way, the boats steam out into the Ohio and start upstream.

Will and Jim were packed on the upper deck of the steamer "City of Memphis" like a box of sardines with their comrades. While the day lasted the boys feasted their eyes on the scenery from either side and enjoyed the first steamboat ride of their lives.

At night they spread their blankets on the deck and laid down to dream of home, but before going to sleep, they had a "talk-fest," as they called it, Jim thinking they must be going to Cincinnati. But Will thought different, and said: "I don't know where we'll land, but I'll bet a hard tack it will be down south somewhere among the secesh."

The next morning when they awoke they found themselves, not on the Ohio, but on the Tennessee river headed down South. "What did I tell you last night, Jim, that we were going to land somewhere in Dixie."

"Say, Will, are you in close touch with Grant that you know what he's going to do?"

"No, but what's a feller got a 'bean' on top of his body, if it isn't to think a little and reason things out somewhat?"

During the day our boat tied up at a landing for the purpose of loading up with cord wood for fuel. Permission was given to the boys to go ashore and stretch their legs. There was a large warehouse there, stored with merchandise.

The owner at once secured a guard to be placed over some barrels of whiskey. In every company there were men who liked strong drinks, and in prowling around they spied these barrels of whiskey, and ways and means were at once started to get some of the fiery stuff. One of the soldiers was directed to go near one of the barrels and while talking with the guard to let his gun drop on the floor, the man underneath would note where the gun struck the floor by the dust loosened up, and the man who had let his gun drop came down and directed just where the end of the barrel of whiskey would be. An auger was procured and a hole was bored through the floor into the barrel of whiskey. The boys stood ready with their canteens and caught the precious stuff (?) as it came down. Not long after quite a number of the soldiers were making merry and showing certain signs of being under the influence of liquor. The officers were puzzled as to how the men secured the liquor and rushed to the guard, accusing him of his failure to properly guard his charge. He denied strenuously that he had permitted any one to touch the barrels. One of the officers leaned against one of the barrels and being empty it toppled over, and the cat was out of the bag. The guard was exonerated, but some of the soldiers who had taken too much of the stuff for their good were arrested and punished. The plotters, however, were not discovered. It is a strange fact that those who liked the fiery liquid, could smell out where it was located and use the most curious ways to obtain it.

On February 6, 1862, in the afternoon, we landed on the eastern bank of the river, and the soldiers were located in camps near by. This being our first camp in Dixie, it was called "Camp Halleck." How it did rain that night and blow, leveling many of our tents.

Many of the boys made light of their mishaps. We pitched our tents near a farm house, and the planter, not knowing our reputation at home for honesty and uprightness, went to our Colonel and asked that a guard be placed around the farmhouse to protect him and his property. The Colonel granted the request, for at this stage of war, orders were very strict about foraging and taking anything from the planters. It fell to the writer's lot to stand guard for two hours that night, during that fearful storm, over some pigs. How digusted he was: the idea of enlisting to fight for "Old Glory" and save the Union, and the first thing he had to do was to guard a lot of dirty pigs that were not half as good as those in his father's farm yard, but "orders is orders," as Jim said, and 'tis a soldier's duty to obey. Strict orders were issued that no trespassing would be permitted and a soldier caught stealing would be severely punished. My two hours of guard duty over those pigs was up at last and I turned them over to another sentinel. During the night a great squawking was heard, and in the early morning the owner of the farm complained to our Colonel that the soldiers had stolen his geese. The Colonel ordered an officer to search each tent to find the stolen geese and the thieves. When the officer came to our tent, he commenced to turn over our blankets and knapsacks. There was one sleepy fellow lying down with his head on his knapsack for a pillow, apparently sound asleep; the officer touched him, but he slept on and one of the boys said: "Don't wake that fellow up, he's been on guard duty all night."

"All right," said the kind-hearted officer and passed out of the tent. How relieved we were when he had gone away, for that sleepy fellow had his head on his knapsack which held the goose. Of course we had goose for breakfast, and it tasted mighty good if it was a "Dixie" goose. Don't ask me who stole it, for

I'll never tell, and my comrades will not tell.

The next morning we took up our line of march toward Fort Henry. The rain had fallen the night before, making the roads very muddy. Many times we had to stop, stack arms, throw off knapsacks and put our shoulders to the wheels of the artillery and help them out of the mud holes. We came to several streams not bridged, but we were enthusiastic in our seeking the enemy and spoiling for a fight. Taking no time to build temporary bridges, we plunged into the water waist deep and pushed ahead. This made me think of what I had read of our Revolutionary fathers "wading swollen streams and toiling through almost impassible barriers to fight for their liberty and rights."

We hadn't come to the fighting yet, but we hoped to do so soon; then we could class ourselves with our forefathers. Now, I smile over the thought I had then when a lad of 18 years, and though you may smile, the thought comes that if we youngsters had not had the spirit of emulating the deeds of our forefathers, where would this grand nation be today?

In the distance the gunboats were hammering away at Fort Henry, and as the sound of the booming cannon came to our ears we wished we were there to attack from the land side. Commodore A. H. Foote, with five gunboats, had attacked the fort and the fight was a most thrilling picture; the whizzing of fragments of bursting shells; the deafening roar of the guns in the fort; the black sides of five gunboats belching fire at every port hole was something to be remembered a lifetime. The fire from the gunboats dismounted seven big guns and brought down the flagstaff, and, together with the bursting of a rifled gun in the fort, created a panic in the enemy's ranks. A shot from the enemy passed through the boiler of the Essex and many were scalded. When the Union tars were told that the enemy had surrendered, a sailor named Breas, who was badly wounded, sprang to his feet saying, "Surrender! I must see that with my own eyes before I die," and then, climbing two short flights of stairs to the deck, he saw a white flag flying over Fort Henry, and shouted, "Glory to God!" sank exhausted on the deck and died that night.

We were tramping along in the mud when a messenger passed along the line announcing the capture of the fort by the gunboats. Some of us cheered, but others were silent and really felt sore at the sailors for their taking of the fort before we had a chance to help them. How foolish we were then. We had enough of fighting ere the war was over, and after the first battle we never begrudged other forces the honor of gaining a victory without our help. Most of the enemy had "skedaddled" to Fort Donelson. Commodore Foote took a small number of prisoners, together with Commander General Tighlman. It was after dark when we reached the outer earthworks, inside of which we camped. Here we spent our second night in Dixie, without any shelter save the blue sky above us. We built large fires and managed to keep fairly comfortable, although it was pretty cold. Will was up very early the next morning, and, having an intense desire to see the inside of the fort, took "French leave" and started in that direction. (A French leave is nothing more than a "pass" taken on your own responsibility.) He found that the fort was situated on a very low piece of land; indeed, it was a swamp, nearly all surrounded by water. The works were well constructed, but whoever selected this as a suitable site for a fort was, Will thought, either insane or knew nothing of modern warfare. Ignorant as Will was of military ways, he said he would not have picked on this place for a fort. Here Will had his first view of the dead and mangled upon the battle field. One of the largest of the cannon had burst while the cannonading was in progress and this carried destruction to all those around the gun, tearing them all to pieces. Will said afterwards: "I shall to my dying day carry that picture in my memory." Now, for the first time, did Will realize the horrors of war. In his eagernes to secure relics he knocked off a large piece of the bursted cannon and with other relics he loaded himself down, but after carrying them for a while he threw them away, thinking it would be a long time ere he returned home, as it surely proved to be. After viewing the destruction on every hand until he was satisfied, Will returned to camp in time to escape being noticed by his officer.

FORT DONELSON

CHAPTER II.

With the fall of Fort Henry, we started toward Fort Donelson. The roads were muddy and the country hilly, making the marching hard work. About 3 o'clock p. m. of February 12, 1862, the distant booming of cannon told us all too plainly that we were near the enemy, and we were urged to greater speed. When within two miles of the fort a group of officers passed us, among them Gen. Grant, Gen. W. H. L. Wallace, Col. Oglesby and others. We were ordered to unsling knapsacks and leave them in company piles, with a guard over them, and then away we went over hills, valleys and ravines, through the woods and dense thickets. After having marched about a mile and a half we were halted, darkness having arrived. The night was very chilly and cold. Our boys had left their knapsacks two miles to the rear and were without blankets. Cold, hungry and disappointed, we shivered during that long, dreary night, and began to realize what an earnest, cruel thing a soldier's life was. But it was our first experience, and we knew nothing about making ourselves comfortable. We learned better after a while and always carried our blankets with us, whether in battle or not. It is the best plan to always have a blanket with you. During the night it rained and turned very cold. We were forbidden to leave the lines, hence could not go back for our blankets. Will gathered up a pile of leaves and crept into them, but this did not keep him warm, and becoming cold he got up and paced back and forth to try to keep warm.

At the first streak of day—February 13, 1862—the enemy bade us good morning by sending us a shell that burst close to our lines, but doing little damage. The boys were mad and, gathering their muskets, said: "Let's show them that we are not to be shot at without returning the compliment,'' but our officers were not ready to give us a chance. The battle was on, however, at other points of the line, and at last we were to have our hearts' desires, namely, of having a shot at the enemy. We were moved shortly to the right and formed in line with our brigade.

About noon our General, W. H. L. Wallace, sent the 48th Illinois to attack what looked like a small redoubt to the left and front of us. This regiment gallantly attacked and fought desperately for some time, but losing their Colonel, they fell back, and then Gen. Wallace ordered the 45th Illinois to go to their aid. Now the time had come for us to show what stuff we were made of; now had come the time to do what we had promised our loved ones at home—to fight gallantly for the dear old flag. The orders of our Colonel were:

''Attention, battalion! Fix bayonets; shoulder arms; right shoulder shift, arms. Forward, march!" and all moved toward the enemy's works over very rough ground. The redoubt of the enemy was on a hill, the ground sloping down toward us, while the trees and brush had been cut down to retard our progress. Presently the bullets began to sing about our heads: *zip, ping, ping,* and as we climbed the hill we were met by a murderous fire of musketry; the men were falling in bunches and the enemy poured into us grape and canister from their cannons.

When we got close enough the order to fire was given, and we boys sent our first lead into the enemy who showed themselves on top of the breastwork. The firing on both sides was brisk, but our Colonel would not let the men advance any farther. He knew we could not climb over the trench in front of the breastworks and scale the works. We fought an hour at great disadvantage, when the order was given to slowly retire. We had smelt powder for the first time and had heard the whiz of the minie-ball, many of our brave comrades making the greatest sacrifice a man can make for his country. They had given their lives for the flag.

The gunboats on the river side of the fort had been doing valiant work, but had suffered badly at the hands of the enemy. The flagship St. Louis, had her steering wheel shattered, the pilot was killed, and Admiral Foote was wounded. The flagstaff was shot away and Captain J. V. Johnston, fastening the flag to his arm, walked the deck and gave the signals.

For the interest of my young readers, I must tell you about Captain Johnston's little boy, Master James Vincent Johnston, aged about 8 years at the time. Captain Johnston's wife and little boy were visiting him on the gunboat when the enemy opened fire from an unseen battery on the shore. The Captain had tied the boy by his mother's side in one of the cabins, but he succeeded in untying himself and ran off among the gunners, where he seemed to take great delight during the excitement. Presently the Captain came along and met the little fellow carrying a pouch of powder. His father was surprised, and asked him where he got his load. The child answered:

"Why, Tommy had his head shotted off over there an' I'm carrying the powder," and he ran to the gun carrying his load.

The Captain let him have his way and little Jimmy was the hero of the battle, and the sailors called him "Admiral Jimmie."

After the unsuccessful attack on the fort we again took our places in the line with our brigade. During the night the cold was intense and the men suffered much; some perished, icicles hanging from the caps of the sentinels. Our grub at this time was very scarce. We learned better later on in the war to always

General Grant examining a prisoner's haversack
at Fort Donelson

carry a good supply of hard tack in our haversacks for just such emergencies.

Towards evening some prisoners were captured and were taken to General Grant, who examined their haversacks and found them well filled with rations. The General reasoned from this fact, that the enemy were preparing to make their escape, which they did try to do the next day.

Soon after dark some of us were detailed to dig trenches and assist in erecting breastworks for the artillery. The Seventh Corporal was detailed to take charge of the squad, but it being so bitter cold he feigned sickness and turned the squad over to Will. He took his place and did the best he could, getting no sleep at all during the night. The next morning Jim asked Will how he liked his job. "Oh," said Will, "the job was all right, but I'll tell you, Jim, I think less of that Seventh Corporal than I did before, because of that little trick of his."

During the night the Confederate Generals held a council of war and decided to mass their troops on our right the next morning, and cut their way out and escape.

Just as the first faint streaks of light came over the hills, so also came the compliments from the enemy, in the shape of iron shells from their cannons. McAllister's battery returned the salutation in earnest and the battle was on again. Saturday, February 15, 1862, the enemy massed 10,000 troops opposite General McClernand's division, on our right, and advanced upon our line, the pickets being fired upon before dawn.

The order, "Fall in," was given and in a few minutes the woods rang with rattle of musketry and the roar of cannon. The enemy were determined to turn our right flank and escape. The battle raged fiercely for an hour and a half, and then came a lull. Colonel Forrest with his dashing cavalry made a charge on our lines at one point and captured one of our batteries. The fighting at other points all along the line that stretched for over three miles was heavy. About 10 o'clock our troops upon the extreme right ran out of ammunition, and Gen. Oglesby's brigade had to fall back.

General Lew Wallace now came up with fresh troops, their cartridge boxes full, and those that had fallen back having now received plenty of cartridges reformed their lines and again took part in the fight to drive the enemy back into their breastworks.

On the left of our lines a charge on the works had been ordered by Gen. Grant, and Gen. C. F. Smith, leading the boys in blue, placed his hat on his swordpoint and holding it aloft, cried out: "This way, boys; come on," and the boys followed their courageous leader amidst a terrible hail of minie-balls and cannon shot. The 2nd, 7th, 12th and 14th Iowa and the 25th Indiana Regiments engaged in this charge, planting their colors on the outer works, the enemy falling back to an inner breastwork. There was more or less fighting all day, but we finally drove the enemy back into their fort and had them cooped up and nearly surrounded.

During the battle in front of our lines, one of our company was wounded and went a few rods to the rear and sat down behind a tree. The Lieutenant Colonel seeing him there and thinking he was skulking went at him fiercely, saying: "Gill, get back into line." Now, Gill was an odd genius, slow of speech and having a peculiar drawl in his manner of speaking, replied: "I guess not, Colonel; I'm wounded."

"Where are you wounded?"

"In the breast, Colonel."

The Colonel still having his doubts, asked where the ball hit him. Gill, raising his finger and covering the track of the bullet, said: "It went skewaggling this a way."

Sure enough, a minie-ball had torn a hole

clear across his breast, making an ugly looking flesh wound. Gill remained behind the tree until told to go and see the surgeon.

It is a fact that many new words were coined during the Civil War, some of them coming into general use and finding place in the dictionaries.

So far I have not seen Gill's new word in the dictionaries, but surely it was a most apt description of how he was wounded.

Another member of our company was taking his coffee from the fire in the early morning when a stray, spent bullet from the enemy struck him in the head and knocked him down. He was taken back a short distance and the surgeon extracted a bullet flattened out and lying just under the scalp. He recovered, but the boys called him "Old bullet-proof skull," or "Old hard head," after that.

CHAPTER III.

That night, as the boys lay in line of battle, they discussed the doings of the day.

"Say, Will, how did you feel to be in battle today?"

"Well, Jim, the greatest strain was waiting in line of battle, either for an advance or to receive the enemy's charge when I could do nothing, and hearing the booming of cannon and rattle of musketry in other parts of the battle field, I felt as though my heart was in my mouth, and there came a desire to run for a place of safety; but after we got into action, amid the smoke, dirt, excitement and noise, I forgot where my heart was and had no desire to run; fear had been displaced by a savage instinct to inflict injury on the enemy."

Many have tried to explain the feeling while on the battlefield, and it is probable that a battle affects men in different ways. However, we think Will's description of the feeling is about right.

Late Saturday night we bivouacked near the firing line without fire and very little to eat. The ground was covered with snow and ice and the weather very cold.

Captain Johnson, of Company F, had his feet frozen so badly he never could wear his boots again, but, instead, wore a pair of large army brogans.

Fatigue parties were detailed to search for and bring in the wounded; this labor extending throughout the night, the surgeons never rested and there was no distinction between the blue and the gray.

As the Union army on this dreary Saturday night rested in bivouac close in front of the enemy's works, the moans of the wounded could be heard, and here and there flickering lights moved through the woods on errands of mercy.

Mother Bickerdike, a nurse with the Union

army, was out on the battle field with her lantern, groping among the dead, stooping down and turning their cold faces towards her, she scrutinized them earnestly, uneasy lest some might be wounded and left to die uncared for. How many poor fellows, sick and wounded, have been ministered to by her loving hands, and the soldiers of the Army of the Tennessee, who loved Mother Bickerdike, have said over and over again, "God bless Mother Bickerdike."

One incident has come down to us which shows how she loved her boys. One morning, visiting one of the wards in a certain field hospital at about 11 o'clock a. m., she found the poor fellows had had no breakfast; the doctor in charge, had not been present to make out the special diet list for each one, he having been out on a spree the night before. The doctor came in just as Mother Bickerdike learned the facts and she went for him.

"You miserable scoundrel; here these men, anyone of them worth a thousand of you, are suffered to starve and die, because you want to be off on a drunk. Pull off your shoulder straps, for you shall not stay in the army a week longer!"

The doctor laughed at her, but within three days she had caused his discharge. He went to General Sherman to be reinstated.

The General said: "Who caused your discharge?"

"Why," said the doctor, hesitatingly, "I suppose it was that woman, Mrs. Bickerdike."

"Oh," said General Sherman. "Well, if it was she, I can do nothing for you; she ranks me."

During the night, while we boys were trying to keep from freezing and wondering what the morrow would bring forth, the Confederate Generals held another council of war, deciding they could not hold out longer against Gen. Grant's army, and would surrender.

Colonel Forrest (who commanded the cavalary) during the council arose and said: "I will not surrender my command or myself," and left the council. During the night, or early morning, he and his command escaped by wading the river on our extreme right, which was unprotected by the Union forces.

Colonel Forrest was a brave man and a terrible fighter, as our troops afterwards learned on numerous occasions.

The two senior Generals of the Confederates turned the command over to Gen. S. B. Buckner, who somewhat scornfully notified his colleagues, that if they proposed to escape they must do so speedily, for after he should open negotiations with General Grant no one would be allowed to leave the fort.

I have always admired General Buckner for declining to leave, claiming as he did, that it was honorable to stay with his soldiers.

During the night or early morning, Gen.

Buckner sent a note, under a flag of truce, to Gen. Grant, asking an armistice to arrange terms of surrender.

Without a moment's hesitation, Gen. Grant wrote the following answer, probably one of the finest specimens of energetic war literature in military history.

"No terms other than an unconditional and immediate surrender can be accepted. I propose to move immediately upon your works."

Upon the receipt of this, Gen. Buckner promptly returned his answer of acceptance.

From this time on during the war, Gen. U. S. Grant was known as "Unconditional Surrender Grant."

Will kept a diary and we are permitted to quote from it:

"Soon after daybreak (Sunday, February 16, 1862) we heard great cheering by the troops along the line and presently orderlys came galloping towards us, swinging their caps and proclaiming the news of the surrender of the fort. Did we shout? Well, if we didn't use our lungs then we never did. Hip! Hip! Hurrah! from every man in blue. The victory was ours and we rejoiced over the fall of the Confederate stronghold."

The Union loss was about 2,400, and the Confederate loss was 2,000 killed and wounded, besides 15,000 prisoners and munitions of war.

Presently the order to march was given and we marched into Fort Donelson with bands playing and colors flying. It was a grand sight, as regiment after regiment poured in with their flags floating gayly in the wind, and the brass bands playing, "Hail Columbia," "Yankee Doodle," etc., in such style as the gazing captives had never heard even in the palmy days of peace.

The Confederates were drawn up in line with their guns thrown down, and with a woebegone, sullen, downhearted look they watched our parading.

A few of them told us they were forced into the army and did their fighting unwillingly. We did not believe a word of it. We marched to the large fort next to the river and planted our colors upon the ramparts and then camped inside the fort. The prisoners were very anxious to know what their fate was to be. They were assured they would be taken north and kept as prisoners of war until exchanged.

Gen. Lew Wallace was the first inside the works, and going to the Confederate headquarters was met by Gen. Buckner, who invited him to breakfast, which invitation was accepted, the bill of fare being coffee and corn bread.

The fall of Fort Donelson was the first great and valuable victory won by the Union armies during the war. When the news flashed through the loyal states, the people went wild with enthusiasm. Salutes were fired, joy bells rung, flags displayed everywhere, and the people asked one another: "Who is this Grant,

Charge of the 8th Missouri and 11th Indiana Regiments, led by General Lew Wallace, at Fort Donelson

and where did he come from?" Before the war closed the people found out who Grant was and what was in him.

There were others in the battle of Donelson, who, afterwards became famous. There was our gallant Illinois soldiers, Colonel John A. Logan, the "Black Eagle" of Egypt; the bluff old Colonel Richard Oglesby, both of whom became Major Generals, and after the war served in the United States Senate from the State of Illinois. Then Gen. Lew Wallace, of Indiana, the noted author of "Ben Hur," and Colonel John A. Rawlins, of Galena, Ill., chief of staff of Gen. Grant, who, afterwards became Secretary of War under Grant, and many others.

In speaking of Colonel Oglesby, we must give you an old story about him which happened while he was in command of the 8th Illinois Regiment. One day while the regiment was in camp, two of the drum corps went into the woods to practice, and, while practicing, a nice fat pig came nosing around. The temptation to the drummers was too great; the pig was caught and slaughtered, but now the thought came to them: "How shall we get into camp without discovery." A happy idea, "Let's put him in the big drum." So the head of the drum was taken off and Mr. Pig safely stowed away, and they arrived at camp. The regiment was on dress parade when they arrived at camp. The Colonel was vexed at their absence, and as soon as he saw them, sternly ordered them to take their places with the music. The drummers did not know what to do, but one of them went up to the Colonel, and, in an under tone, told him the situation, winding up with, "We 'low, Colonel, to bring the best quarter over to your mess." The Colonel thundered out: "Sick, hey! Why didn't you say so at first. Go to your quarters, of course. Battalion right face, to your quarters, march." The Colonel had fresh pork for supper.

After the fall of Fort Donelson, the people of the North believed that it would be but a short time until the rebellion would be put down, and we boys could go home. Captain Johnson wrote home: "I believe it won't be over three months now until the rebellion will be squelched and we shall be permitted to go home."

Yes, we boys thought then that we had broken the backbone of the rebellion, and that the war would soon be over. How badly mistaken we were history proves. It was but the beginning of a terrible four years of battle and bloodshed ere the end came.

SHILOH

CHAPTER IV.

We remained in Fort Donelson for a little over two weeks. The weather was miserably wet, cold and disagreeable all the time, and the boys wondered why we didn't move on, and were getting impatient.

"Say, Will, how long do you think we are going to stay in this miserable old hole?"

"I don't know, Jim; but I'll bet you a hardtack that we will be marching within three days."

"You seem to be so cocksure, I wonder if Gen. Grant has told you anything."

"No, Jim," said Will," he hasn't told me anything, nor do I believe he has told anybody what he is going to do, for I believe he is one of those silent men that talk very little."

"Well, what makes you so certain we are going to move soon?"

"Oh, I just put two and two together and

add them up and it makes four. So, when I see them getting the horses and mules all shod and loading up our commissary and ammunition wagons to the top, I just say, that's two and two and that makes four, and so we march."

"Well, Will, you are a curious fellow, and if we do move soon, I'll say you are one of the smartest fellows in camp."

"Oh, shaw! that isn't smartness, that's just a little common horse sense put to work."

Will's prophecy came true, and in three days the victorious army under Grant started again for the Tennessee River. On March 24, 1862, we landed at Pittsburg Landing on the west side of the Tennessee River, and went into camp about two miles southwest of the landing.

At this place Gen. Grant was assembling an army to march on to Corinth and attack Gen. Johnson's Confederate forces. Our troops had been located with a view to convenience, rather than in a compact line facing an enemy. The great gaps between the different divisions indicated that the officers did not expect a general attack; still, I cannot see how they could have lulled themselves into this belief. To show that there had been signs of an enemy hovering near our camps, I will copy from an old diary kept by me at that time. I had forgotten this incident until reading it lately when it all came back to me as vividly as though of recent occurrence. "April 4th. Today I am on guard as Sergeant of the Second Relief.

"At night the troops were ordered out in line of battle, word having come that an attack had been made upon our outer line of pickets. Our regiment moved to the right and in front of our camp.

"My relief was on duty some little distance in the woods. Soon after the alarm was given, I received orders from the officer of the day to take off my sentinels and order each man to his respective company for duty. I proceeded to obey orders and had passed about half way 'round giving orders to my men, when, groping through the underbrush, I came to a sentinel whom I could not see very well because of the extreme darkness, and supposing he was one of my guard, I gave the order, and was just starting away when the sentinel called out sharply, 'Halt.' I had given the countersign before, so I turned and wanted to know what was up. He informed me that he was on picket duty and wanted to know who I was and what I wanted. I explained the situation to him, which seemed satisfactory, and I was permitted to go. Retracing my steps I found my own guard line. I had, in the darkness, stumbled into the picket line of another regiment and was ordering in soldiers with whom I had no business. The sentinel was all right and determined to do his duty, for as he cried *halt* he raised his musket, pulled the hammer and was ready to shoot, but as an obedient soldier I obeyed his command

and halted, and in so doing escaped being shot by one of our own soldiers. The troops were kept in line of battle until 10 o'clock p. m., when the officers, believing it to be a 'scare,' ordered the soldiers to their respective camps."

This incident tends to show that the enemy was hovering near our immediate front.

Calling a few years ago upon my old Colonel, Gen. John E. Smith, of the United States army (now deceased), and talking over some of our battles, I asked him about some feature of the battle of Shiloh, to which he replied: "Well, Wilbur, after reading all the histories and articles published on the battle of Shiloh, I am in doubt whether I was there at all." But he was there, and by reason of his courage and skill merited the promotion he afterwards received.

The Generals and officers have had almost a monopoly since the war, in telling how such and such a battle was fought, and the magazines have been filled with the story of General

So and So winning this battle and losing another. The Sergeants, Corporals and the privates who did the hard fighting in the ranks have not been heard from very much. It's about time we had our say, so that the future historian may gather facts from the ranks as well as from the officers, and thus be able to make a complete history.

The ground at Shiloh is quite uneven and very woody, with here and there a field or "clearing."

There was a little log church near Gen. Sherman's camp, called "Shiloh," where the battle commenced, and the great battle of April 6 and 7, 1862, has gone down in history as the battle of Shiloh.

The Confederate army had approached our lines very quietly within two miles; the beating of drums had been forbidden and every precaution taken to keep the Union army from knowing of their presence. The sound of "taps" in the Union army at 9 o'clock Saturday night was distinctly heard in the enemy's camp, but we hard no "taps" from their army.

Never did a morning open with brighter, happier prospects than did that Sunday morning of April 6, 1862. Never did the sun beam forth, shedding its golden rays on a devoted, unsuspecting army, with more loveliness. Never was a wilderness made more cheerful and inviting by the innocent chirpings and songs of myriads of warbling songsters, perched among the many trees of our camp, little dreaming of the approaching dangers which was destined so soon to be drenched with human blood.

Will, being an early riser from force of habit, having been raised on a farm, had been up long enough to have eaten his breakfast, while Jim, his bunk mate, was just coming out of his tent, when the rattle of musketry was heard out in front to the southwest.

"Will, what was that noise off there, rumbling of the wagons?'' inquired Jim.

''No, Jim, I think its musketry firing.''

''Oh, said John Shannon. ''You are away off. There isn't any enemy within miles of us.''

While the boys were debating, the long roll sounded at headquarters, ''bur-r-r-r rat-tat-tat-bur-r-r.''

The boys were astonished and startled, but they knew then what the noise they had heard meant, and each man jumping for his musket and cartridge box, fell into line without the word of command. In less than five minutes the regiment was in line ready for orders. This was about 6 o'clock in the morning. After waiting impatiently for some fifteen or twenty minutes, we received orders from Gen. McClernand, commanding our division, to move to the left a little and out in front to support Gen. Sherman's division, whose troops were the first to receive an attack from the enemy, which was so fierce, desperate and sudden that some of his troops were surprised and thrown into a panic. They rallied, however, and checked the foe. Soon heavy musketry and cannonading were opened on our immediate left. Again we were moved to the left to aid the troops now in mortal combat, and taking our position in the woods we awaited the enemy.

Now, out of the forest in front march the gray line of battle, four columns deep, with arms at a right shoulder shift. On the columns march, without a break in their ranks, carrying a flag which appears to be the stars and stripes.

When they got near enough for our soldiers to open fire on them, we begin to get uneasy and want to commence firing. The men in the ranks realize that the first volley is needed now to check the oncoming foe. Jim was one of the nervous fellows and said to Will: "What does it mean? Why don't our officers give the command to fire?"

Will replied: "You know the orders are not

to fire until the command is given." But even Will believed we were making a mistake in not firing, now that the enemy was in range.

The strain for those few minutes becomes too intense. A few of the men commence to shoot without orders, when an officer rushes down the line shouting: "Cease firing, those are our troops."

Two or three men of Will's company, who had no fear of an officer, and who now at this supreme moment seemed to know more than their officers, had been firing, among them Jim, who answered the officer: "The hell they are! You will find out pretty d—d soon they are not."

Will said: "Better obey the officer, Jim; but I can't blame you for swearing a little just now." The soldiers obeyed and ceased firing.

Five minutes of terrible suspense, with that gray line advancing nearer and nearer; then suddenly a most destructive volley of musketry was poured into our ranks, and our men fell like autumn leaves. Did we wait for orders to "fire?" No! Every man opened fire, loading and discharging his gun as rapidly as possible, the roar of musketry from either side being terrific. The underbrush is mowed down by bullets. Men are shot in several places in the body in a moment. The dead lie where they fall, and the wounded drag themselves to the rear. Our rapid firing has now checked the onward march of the enemy in our immediate front, but the regiment and battery upon our right were not so fortunate, and with unearthly yells the enemy charge the battery. The gunners fight like heroes, manning their guns until bayoneted. The boys thought it was Schwartz's battery. The horses all being killed or wounded the cannon could not be taken away and were captured. It is related of an officer of this battery that, later in the day, he rode up to Gen. Grant, and touching his cap, said: "Sheneral,

I vants to make one report. Schwartz's battery is took."

"Ah," said the General; "how did that happen?"

"Vell, you see, Sheneral, de secesh come up in front of us and dey flank us and so Schwartz's battery was took."

"Well, sir," said the General; "you spiked the guns, of course?"

"Vat!" exclaimed the officer; "schpike dem new guns. It would spoil dem."

The regiment that supported this battery failed to stand up to the rack, and when the charge was made beat a retreat too soon. Our right flank was now about to be turned by the enemy, and the order was given to fall back a short distance. We fell back about two hundred yards and the lines were again formed. At this first engagement of the day we left a large number of our boys to sleep their last sleep. Again the battle was on, and the terrible work of destruction went on all along the line. The screaming shells and whizzing bullets carried death and wounds wherever they went. The line of battle stretched for a distance of two miles and raged with fury the entire length, the enemy massing their forces at certain points and pushing the Union troops back, then attempting to flank the regiment to the right or left. Such were the tactics used by Generals Johnson and Beauregard, and they were well managed, indeed.

CHAPTER V.

One position after another was taken, and from each we were driven, or had to fall back for fear of being flanked.

The third position our brigade took was on the brow of a small hill, where we held the enemy at bay for two hours, at one time charging and driving them for a quarter of a mile, then falling back for lack of support on our right.

A Confederate officer has said of Shiloh: "The Confederate assaults were made by rapid charges along the line. They were repeatedly checked and often repulsed. Sometimes counter charges drove them back, but whether in assault or recoil, both sides saw their bravest soldiers fall in frightful numbers." This officer's statement is true to the letter.

We then took a new position on the edge of an open field. For an hour we listened to and were in the midst of an artillery duel. At times the battle seemed to die out, and all was still in our immediate vicinity; but this stillness only portended the fiercer the fight when again commenced.

About 3 o'clock our cartridges began to run low, and we borrowed each of the other until all was gone; we were holding the enemy, but now our guns were silent. What a helpless man a soldier is in a battle with no ammunition. We marched to the rear left in front in search of cartridges, and none too soon either, for a troop of the enemy's cavalry were seen on our right, trying to get in our rear and take us prisoners. We had not gone far when we met a line of fresh troops, of whom we begged cartridges, but the caliber was not the right size for our Enfield rifles and we could not use them, and we started on again hunting for cartridges, the enemy pressing us so hard that the Captain of the rear company went rushing up to the Colonel, exclaiming breathlessly:

"My God, Colonel, they are not fifty yards from my company, and we haven't a shot to defend ourselves."

"Keep cool," said the Colonel, "and don't say anything, the enemy don't know we are out of ammunition, and we will come out all right yet."

We had not gone far when we met a wagon loaded with cartridges. Caliber 58. Did you ever see a hungry lot of men wade into a bang-up dinner?

Will was the first to mount the wagon and rip open one of the boxes in quick order, the men scrambling up into the wagon, and crying out: "Give me some, give me more!" The cartridge boxes and pockets were filled in short order. We then took our position on the right of our brigade, supporting a battery.

The enemy soon opened on us with a heavy artillery fire, and either having the best guns or gunners silenced our cannon. The horses were killed, men wounded and killed, but the infantry held the line; we felt strong and courageous now, with plenty of cartridges. The men began to realize that this line must be held though every man fall.

There was one place on the battle line of Sunday which was occupied by the gallant troops under Gen. W. H. L. Wallace, and who held the enemy at bay for a long time, the Confederates charging this place several times and being repulsed each time. "Its a regular hornet's nest," said one of the Confederate officers, and the spot as located by the United States Commissioners of the Shiloh National Park, bears the name, "Hornet's Nest," at the present time. It was at this point that the brave and beloved Gen. W. H. L. Wallace received his mortal wound. To the east of the "Hornet's Nest," a short distance, is the place where Commanding General of the Confeder-

The fight in the peach orchard at Shiloh

ate army, Gen. Albert Sidney Johnston, was killed. I believe that Gen. Johnston was the greatest General of the Confederate army, and many others agree with me.

A little to the rear of Gen. Wallace's troops was a small pond of water. The wounded soldiers crawled to this pond to slake their thirst and bathe their wounds, and so many washed their wounds in this pond that the water looked like a pool of blood, and it was called the "Bloody Pond."

The pond is still there, and has a fence around it, with a tablet giving its name, "Bloody Pond," and captured cannon surround it.

The Union forces that were left were now concentrated in a much shorter line, with no gaps susceptible to a flank movement of the enemy.

As the sun went down in the west I noticed it looked as red as blood, indicative of the bloody work we had been doing on that holy Sabbath day. Night again brooded o'er us.

With the awful carnage of blood and destruction strewn over two miles, with thousands of killed and wounded on both sides, no doubt both armies were glad that darkness closed the terrible struggle, for the day at least. Our Orderly Sergeant of our company called the roll and out of 55 that started in the morning, 31 answered "here," and with the exception of two or three, the rest had been killed or wounded.

We bivouacked on the firing line, the rain coming down during the night wetting us through and through. Our company was with others detailed for picket duty that night between 10 and 12 o'clock, and stationed about two hundred yards in front of our line.

Will was posted near a big tree. The night was pitch dark, and having had nothing to eat since morning he was tired and sleepy. But, realizing the duty of a soldier never to fall asleep on the picket line, he tried in every way to keep awake. In telling his experience afterwards to

Jim, he said: "I never worked harder. I pulled my hair and bit my lips to keep awake. About 11 o'clock I heard the cracking of twigs in front of me. The darkness was intense. I could see nothing, but sleepiness was gone then. I listened intently. On it came, something, somebody making straight for me. I waited, with musket ready to fire, until I thought it time to make the challenge, and then cried out: 'Halt; Who goes there?' He halted, and out of the darkness came a voice saying:

" 'I am wounded and want to get to a surgeon.' I was not satisfied with this. He might be an enemy trying to capture the sentinels, and the enemy then would make a night attack on our sleeping army in the rear. So I plied him with questions as to his regiment, brigade and division, to which he answered in such a manner that he convinced me he was telling the truth, and I told him to advance. He came hobbling along with a broken ramrod of a cannon for a crutch, shot through the leg. I called the Sergeant of the Guard: 'Sergeant of the Guard, Post No. 6,' and the next sentinel took up the cry and pretty soon the Sergeant came and I turned the poor fellow over to be taken to the Surgeon."

All things have an end. Twelve o'clock came, and, being relieved, we returned to the sleeping line, and, throwing ourselves on the ground, we at once fell asleep. All night the surly gunboats kept up a deadly fire on the enemy in front of our left.

Twice during the night I awoke, and could hear the groans and cries of the wounded lying out there on that bloody field. Some cried for water, others for some one to come and help them. Many years have passed since that terrible day and night, yet when my mind reverts to that time, I can hear those poor fellows crying for water. God heard them, for the heavens were opened and the rain came.

CHAPTER VI.

In the evening of April 6 a few of Gen. Buell's troops had arrived and were placed in position. During the night the boats brought the balance of Buell's army across the Tennessee River and they were in line of battle ere the break of day.

Volumes have been written about the battle of Shiloh. Some think Buell's army saved us. Of course, they helped to win the second day's battle; still there is nothing to prove that Gen. Grant's army would not have won without their assistance on the next day.

Let me quote what I wrote over fifty years ago, when it was fresh in my mind:

"Some think it was Buell's army that saved the army of Gen. Grant from total destruction. I think otherwise, and my reason is this: we had been driven back so near the river that our lines were concentrated as before they were scattered. During the night Gen. Grant and his aides had perfected their line of battle, and Gen. Lew Wallace's division had arrived from Crump's Landing, and every man left in the line knew that to retreat another foot meant total annihilation, and the words: 'We must whip them in the morning,' were upon every man's lips."

The enemy was badly hurt, and Gen. Grant knew it and felt confident that victory must be ours on the morrow.

The morning light had scarcely come on the 7th of April when the roar of artillery announced the opening of the second day's battle. The command, "Forward," was given and the entire line moved forward. We were the aggressors today, and made the first attack.

Fighting continued steadily, the enemy yielding every foot with great reluctance, stubbornly holding their ground, until 12 o'clock, when a general charge was made, and the tide of battle was turned in favor of the Union forces.

During this charge, Will fell to the ground, thinking he was shot through the leg, for it hurt so badly he couldn't stand up; he pulled up his trousers to see where the minie-ball had struck him, to find that the ball had only grazed his shinbone, cutting a nice clean hole through his pants, but not bringing a drop of blood. Will was disgusted, that he should fall out with just a bruised shinbone, and jumping up he went limping after his company.

By 3 o'clock Gen. Beauregard, who was now in command of the Confederate forces, gave the order for a retreat. They kept up a fight to cover their retreat until night, but when darkness came we were in possession of our old camps, where we bivouacked, filled as they were with the dead of both armies. We had no difficulty in sleeping well, even though the silent dead lay all about us. The dead do not disturb us; it is the living we should be afraid of. We built fires and cooked our frugal meal, and, after eating, we gathered 'round the camp fire and recounted the deeds of valor done during the great battle, speaking kind words of our brave comrades who had fallen.

A few Sibley tents, torn and riddled by shot and shell, were all we had left. I lost my shirts, blankets, letters from home, my testament (mother's gift) and a picture of the "girl I left behind me." I was more indignant over the loss of my girl's picture then I was over the other articles.

On Tuesday I was detailed with others to bury the dead lying within our camp and a distance of two hundred yards in advance. I had charge of digging the grave, if a trench over sixty feet long and four feet deep, can be called a grave.

The weather was hot, and most of the dead had been killed early Sunday morning, and dissolution had already commenced. The soldiers gathered the bodies up and placed them in wagons, hauling them near to the trench, and piling them up like cord wood.

We were furnished with plenty of whiskey, and the boys believed that it would have been impossible to have performed the job without it.

When the grave was ready, we placed the bodies therein, two deep; the father, brother, husband and lover, all to lie till Gabriel's trumpet shall sound. All the monument reared to those brave men was a board, nailed to a tree at the head of the trench, upon which I cut with my pocket knife, the words: "125 rebels."

We buried our Union boys in a separate trench, and on another board were these words: "35 Union." Many of our men had been taken away and buried separately by their comrades. It was night when we finished the task, some of the squad, "half seas over" with liquor, but they could not be blamed, for it was a hard job. The next day we burned the dead horses and mules.

A few words about the great battle of Shiloh, as an old veteran views it, as well as some words deduced from history.

It has often been told that the enemy surprised us at Shiloh; that the men were asleep in their tents and were even bayoneted there. This most certainly is erroneous. The Confederate officers report that early Sunday morning, while they were planning the attack, their discussion was abruptly brought to an end by the Union out posts commencing an attack on them.

Our soldiers were *not surprised* in the sense of being taken off their guard.

It was a surprise in the sense, that Gen. Grant and his officers did not expect an attack in force by the enemy, or if they did, they made a great mistake in not being prepared. The fact remains, we were not ready to receive the enemy; not a shovelfull of earth had been thrown up for protection, and the several divisions were scattered so as not to form a continuous battle line.

If mistake it was on the part of Gen. Grant, he profited by it, for such a thing did not happen ever afterward. That the first day's battle of Shiloh was a stubborn and desperate battle cannot be denied. Badeau, in his military history of Gen. Grant, says: "For several hours of the first day there was as desperate fighting as was ever seen on the American Continent, and that, in proportion to the number engaged, equaled any contest during the rebellion."

Gen. W. T. Sherman said: "I never saw such terrible fighting afterward."

Gen. Grant has said: "Shiloh was the severest battle fought in the west during the war, and but few in the east equaled it for hard, determined fighting." Again he says in his Memoirs, speaking of Shiloh: "I saw an open field the second day, over which the Confederates had made repeated charges, so covered with dead that it would have been possible to walk across the clearing in any direction, stepping on dead bodies without the foot touching the ground."

Gen. McClernand and his division have never received their just meed of praise for his and their part in the battle of Shiloh.

Gen. Grant in his later life says this: "The heaviest loss sustained by the enemy was in front of Sherman's and McClernand's divisions."

The official records show that on April 5, 1862, Gen. Grant had 39,830 men and officers for the first day's battle, and Gen. Johnston of the Confederates had 43,968 when we started the battle of Shiloh.

The loss of the Confederates was 24 1-3 per cent; the loss of Grant's five divisions present for duty on Sunday was 26¾ per cent. The loss of the Army of the Tennessee under Grant at Shiloh was 10,944; the loss of the Army of the Ohio under Buell was 2,103. Only a few regiments of Buell's army got into action late in the evening of the first day. Total Union loss 13,047, but this includes 2,314 Union prisoners of Gens. Prentiss' and Wallace's divisions; the loss of the Confederates was 10,699.

I remember no amusing incidents during the battle, save that of one of my company, who was shot through the mouth in such a way as to knock out all of his front teeth. He was a German, who spoke English brokenly, and swore like a trooper; he would spit blood and then curse the enemy with great vehemence, and loading his gun and firing, would exclaim: "D— 'em, dey tinks dey vill spile me so I can't eat hard tack, d— 'em, I'll show dem!" And so he fought while his comrades cheered him on.

It has been said that war is grand and heroic; that fighting is a glorious thing; so it is to read about, but the veterans of fifty years ago have seen war; they know what a horrible thing it is, and I believe that every old veteran who has stood in the battle front, has it in his heart to say: "God grant that wars may cease, and that universal peace may come to this world of ours."

Shiloh was a terrible battle, and now after fifty years have slipped by, I sit in my easy chair and occasionally dream of the past. I seem to hear again as vividly as then, the booming of cannon, the rattle of musketry and the whiz of the minie-ball, amid the cries and groans of my comrades who touched elbows with me, and I ask myself: "Can it be? Was I there, or is it a wild fancy of the brain?" The scenes come too vividly before my memory to doubt it, and I thank God that I was able with my comrades to bear a humble part in saving to those who come after us, this grand nation, and in helping to perpetuate but one flag, the Stars and Stripes—the "Heaven-born banner"—to float over a reunited land and people.

CHAPTER VII.

Before leaving my story of the battle of Shiloh, it will interest the reader to peruse the following account of a visit of some of the participants in the battle, just 47 years after.

The National Association of the Survivors of the Battle of Shiloh held their annual reunion on the battle field of Shiloh, April 6 and 7, 1909. Sixty-six veterans, with their wives and sons and daughters, boarded the steamer "Santillo" at St. Louis, Mo., April 2, 1909, and started for Pittsburg Landing, Tenn. On the morning of April 6, 1909, we landed at Pittsburg Landing, Tenn. Upon the bluff is the National Cemetery, where 4,000 Union soldiers lie buried, most of the head stones bearing the name "Unknown." It is a beautiful cemetery, overlooking the Tennessee River. The farmers from the surrounding country were there with their hacks and carryalls ready to be engaged for a reasonable sum to take the Northern visitors all over the battle field. Our party secured a rancher with a big wagon drawn by a pair of lazy mules (our objective point being the camp of the regiment of which we were members), over fine made, drained roads, and although it had rained heavily the night before, the roads were dry and clear of mud. We found a National Park of nearly 4,000 acres, laid out with roads in every direction; we found monuments everywhere, as well as markers and tablets, denoting the camp of every regiment and different positions held by each regiment and battery in the great battle of April 6 and 7, 1862. Great credit is due the Park Commissioners and Major D. W. Reed (of the 12th Iowa Regiment), Secretary and Historian, for their magnificent work in making this beauty spot in Tennessee. Monuments have been erected by the different states in honor of their troops taking part in the battle. The South have also erected monuments to the memory of the Confederate troops. The Alabama state monument was dedicated on April 7, 1909, both northern and southern men and women participating. The Daughters of the Confederacy of Alabama had sent flowers and a request that the ladies from the North would place them upon the monument, which the Chicago, Iowa and South Dakota ladies did. A prayer was offered and Capt. Irwin, an ex-Confederate, made an address, and he was followed by a Union veteran, eulogizing "Old Glory." Then a young man from the South spoke, saying among other things that he was glad he lived today instead of forty-seven years ago, for now, if the United States were called to a war, the North and South would go side by side, defending their common country. And then the company sang "Nearer, My God, to Thee."

The two days at Shiloh battle field were filled with intense interest to all who were present, especially the veterans who took part in the battle; and where it happened that two or more members of the same regiment were present they would hunt up their camp ground and then find the different positions they held in the battle line of those days, and standing on the same ground as then, live in memory again the terrible scenes of the long ago. The battle line of April 6 and 7, 1862, is about three miles in length and we visited most every part of the field, including the most noted places, viz.: the "Hornet's Nest" and the "Bloody Pond."

To those of our party who wended their way to Shiloh church, where the battle began, a unique experience awaited us. On April 6 (there being about twenty-five from the boat present), upon coming in sight of the church, we beheld the citizens of the surrounding country, with their wives and children, gathered from miles around. The Albert Sidney Johnston Camp of Confederate Veterans were holding their semi-annual meeting in the church, there being present probably twenty-five veterans. We were met by the veterans of the Confederate army with a glad shake and a cordial invitation to remain to dinner with them, which was accepted, and we did enjoy their fried chicken and all the other good things. The dinner was eaten with the sauce of reminiscences and repartee between the blue and the gray. We will give you one little incident in which the Union veteran seemed to get the worst of it. Noticing the leanness of the ex-Confederates, the Union veteran said: "Johnnie, how is it all you fellows look so lean, as though you hadn't enough to eat?" The ex-Confederate, on a wooden leg, made quick reply: "Well, Yank, you see it's this way. You-uns shot us onto crutches and we-uns shot you-uns on the pension roll." After many a joke and story of the battle, the people adjourned to the church for services, the church being filled. Gen. Basil

Duke, one of the Shiloh Park Commissioners, gave a fine address, giving his experience in the battle of Shiloh, where he was wounded. He was in Morgan's command of the Confederate army. Among other things he said:

"We fought in the Civil War for the cause we thought was right. We believed the rights guaranteed to us under the constitution were being taken away from us, and you must admit that our love for our homes and property is as dear to us of the South as it is to you of the North. The people of the North believed that to divide the United States would destroy this Nation. Time has proved under the providence of God that the judgment of the North was correct, for had we succeeded in establishing the Confederate States of America, no doubt later on other states would have felt aggrieved on some question and would have seceded, and in time, had our cause won, this nation would have been divided into a great many small principalities governing themselves. Now the issues for the weal of this great Nation are as dear to us of the South as you of the North."

Gen. Duke closed his address by saying that: "We all rejoice at the fraternal feelings now existing between the North and the South, and hope that ever these bonds of love and good will between us may grow and cement us together, stronger and stronger, and we shall continue to prosper and enjoy the rights and privileges of this great Nation."

W. F. Crummer, of Chicago, Ill., on behalf of the boys in blue and their friends, responded, contrasting the scenes of 47 years ago with those of today. He said in part: "It was a beautiful Sabbath morning, April 6, 1862. The birds were singing among the trees and nature was putting forth her verdure of green, when suddenly the booming of cannon, the shrieking of shells and the rattle of musketry heralded the beginning of one of the most terrible battles of the Civil War. I will not take the time to relate all my experiences of that battle, but simply say this, that when, on Monday evening, we had regained our camp, we found a few Sibley tents all riddled with shot and shell, and while you, ex-Confederates here, had possession of our camp you took my knapsack, blanket, the testament my mother gave me, which I hope you read and profited thereby. You are welcome to that, but one thing you took made me feel badly, and that was the picture of the girl I left behind me, and I am here today to ask you to return that picture. The scene of that awful field of carnage and bloodshed changes. Today, after 47 years have rolled by, the birds are singing in the trees and nature is putting forth its green as then, and all is peaceful, and instead of cannon and bullets greeting us you meet us with open hands and extend to us a cordial greeting and your bountiful hospitality. Our hearts are moved and we thank you most heartily. We rejoice with you that today we know no North, no South, no East, no West, but a reunited country, with one flag and one nation, the grandest Nation on the earth. We trust that we shall always remain a happy and prosperous people, both North and South, working together for the good of the entire country. The feeling of good fellowship shown us today indicates that we are one in spirit and love for our Nation. May we all so live that when the roll is called up yonder we may answer 'Here,' and enter into the heavenly land our God has prepared for us. Again thanking you for your most kindly greeting and hospitality, I bid you Godspeed until we meet again."

The meeting was dismissed in a novel manner. All rose and, shaking hands, sang as they marched around the church, to a Southern melody: "It's All Over Now; It's All Over Now," and with many a "Come and see us again," the veterans and their friends from the North bade their Tennessee friends a hearty good bye.

VICKSBURG

CHAPTER VIII.

A half of a century has passed since the memorable Vicksburg campaign of the Civil War began in the year 1863.

It was my lot to take part in the Vicksburg campaign, and, in giving some reminiscences of that siege, I must speak from the standpoint of a soldier of the 45th Illinois Regiment, Gen. Logan's division in Gen. McPherson's 17th Army Corps, being a part of Gen. Grant's army. Before taking you to the actual siege we must carry you with the army from Milliken's Bend on the Louisiana shore above Vicksburg round on the west side of the Mississippi River to Bruinsburg, 70 miles below Vicksburg, and tell you of the marches and battles we had before we entered the city. In the spring of 1863 we find Gen. Grant and his army of 30,000 men encamped at Milliken's Bend. We could not cross the river at that point and attack Vicksburg from the north, inasmuch as a large portion of that country was an impassable swamp. The first plan devised was to cut a canal to the west, thereby changing the current of the river, by which it was proposed to carry troops, forage and ammunition by transports south of Vicksburg, but this scheme proved ineffectual and was abandoned. Where Vicksburg stands, the cliffs rise abruptly from the water's edge 200 feet. Twenty-eight heavy guns were mounted on the river front, all of which had a plunging fire. Our gunboats could not elevate their guns to do them any damage. Vicksburg was impregnable from the north and the river front. Jeff Davis said: "Vicksburg is the Gibralter of America." By the way, speaking of Jeff Davis reminds me he had a plantation not far from Vicksburg. Soon after the Yankees reached that vicinity, Jeff's slaves deserted him, bag and baggage, and a queer lot of contrabands they were, indeed.

Notice the daring plan of Gen. Grant, namely, to take his army around on the Louisiana shore to a point south of Vicksburg, cross the river, cut loose from his base of supplies and enter the enemy's country.

Gen. Grant devised the plan to have Admiral Porter's gunboats and several steamboats, loaded with rations and ammunition, run the batteries at Vicksburg and be ready to transport the army across the river. The first intimation the rank and file had of such a thing was a notice that our Colonel received one day from the Commanding General: that volunteers were wanted to man the steamboats; to act as firemen, engineers, pilots, etc. The Adjutant called the regiment into line, and the Colonel explained what was wanted. He told the soldiers of the dangerous undertaking; that in all probability the steamers would be riddled with shot and shell and many might perish. Notwithstanding all this, if there were any who would volunteer for this service, let them step three paces to the front. Almost the entire regiment stepped to the front. There was one Lieutenant who did not step to the front. Suffice it to say he was never promoted. The reason is obvious. The Colonel then told the Captains to select those who had had some experience on the river, and enough men were found to man a hundred steamers. There was one of those brave volunteers of our regiment—Charlie Evans—who held to the pilot wheel, when a cannon ball went crashing through the pilot house, driving pieces of timber against him with such force that he never fully recovered, and a few years after we buried him at Galena, Ill. Now the boats are loaded and manned by those brave boys from the Northern prairies. All is ready, the night is propitious, the signal is given and Admiral Porter's flotilla of gunboats and steamers start down the river on the 16th day of April, 1863, to run that storm of fire and iron hail. The enemy endeavored to send those boats and their heroic crews to "Davy Jones' Locker" that night, but with the exception of one boat, the "Henry Clay," they finally passed through. For two hours and forty minutes the fleet was under fire. Every transport was struck and disabled. For eight miles the enemy's cannon hurled shot at them, but the loss of men was small in killed and wounded. Now the gunboats and steamboats have run the rebel batteries and are below the city ready to transport the troops and cannon from the west bank of the river to the east.

Prior to the running of the batteries, many of the troops had marched down on the Louisiana side of the river to Hard Times and Bruinsburg, and were waiting for the boats to arrive, with much anxiety, fearful that they would not stand the awful hammering the enemy would give them. The first to show up was the burning wreck of the "Henry Clay." As it floated by an old southern man whose magnificent mansion bordered the Mississippi River, rubbed his hands in glee, exclaiming, "Where are your gunboats now? Vicksburg has put an end to them all." Not long after his jubilant remark the gunboats appeared coming down the river, and presently the whole fleet hove in sight; then the boys, turning to the haughty Southerner, said: "Did Vicksburg put an end to them all?" The old man was too mad to endure the taunts, and turning away, hid himself. The next day he set fire to his own home rather than allow it to shelter his fancied enemies.

About this time there was excitement in Richmond and Washington. The Confederate government was amazed that their "Gibralter" should have been passed by the "Yankee" fleet of gunboats. At Washington, consternation took hold of the officers at the war office. Gen.

Grant had not informed Gen. Halleck of his plans as to the capture of Vicksburg. Halleck was angry and sent a dispatch ordering Gen. Grant to turn back, but the dispatch failed to reach its destination. There had been a determined effort made at Washington by some Senators and Governors and friends of other Generals, to have Grant removed from his command; but President Lincoln said to them: "I rather like the man; I think we'll try him a little longer." So, because of the faith of Lincoln in Grant's ability, it became possible for him to make that most remarkable campaign and capture of Vicksburg. I believe it is a fact, that now, in the military schools of Europe, the military campaign of Gen. Grant at Vicksburg is studied and considered by authorities as one of the most daring and brilliantly executed movements in modern warfare.

Now for the campaign as seen from a soldier's view. The army has been conveyed across the river. The enemy falls back to Port

Gibson, burning the bridges across the Bayou Pierre. The loss of the bridges does not delay the army very long, for we are supplied with boats or pontoons; with these, in addition to lumber from fences, houses and barns, a bridge is soon built. After crossing the pontoon bridge we soon encountered the enemy at Thompson Hill or Port Gibson. A sharp fight ensues, but the enemy is soon routed and retreats. During our fight at Thompson Hill we had with us that day a Congressman from the North. He had a horse and was riding with our Colonel when the quick rattle of musketry in our front was heard. The order was quickly given and we were moving forward in line of battle. Presently the usual noisy introduction of the sharp crack of the musket and the whiz of the minie-ball opened the exercises. There was a deep ravine a little in our rear. The Congressman or his horse was very tired and remained in the ravine until he heard the wild cheer of our victorious charge, when he came out of that ravine on the gallop, swinging his hat and shouting: "Give it to 'em, boys." It was safe then. But you couldn't blame him much. He wasn't getting the enormous sum of $13 per month to be shot at. A Congressman's salary didn't justify the sacrifice of being riddled with bullets.

Three days' rations are issued to the soldiers and this we are told must sustain us for the next five days. The march is then resumed. On May 12th, at 11 o'clock, we meet the enemy, 5,000 strong, at Raymond, and the fight is opened by the artillery and a sharp battle is fought. The enemy charge our lines, but are repulsed, the fighting continuing until about 2 o'clock p. m., when the order for a charge is given and forward with a cheer the boys go, the enemy breaking and retreating. We occupy the town of Raymond that night. The dead are buried; the wounded are cared for and by daybreak the next morning we are on the march, headed for Jackson, Miss., to clean out Gen. Johnston, and his army that he has concentrated at that place. Our rations are getting short, but the country affords us a fair supply of some things, such as fresh pigs, chickens and vegetables, which we take as a matter of crippling the enemy as well as to satisfy the hungry boys in blue. Our march begins at 4 o'clock in the morning. One day we marched all day in the drizzling rain and at night when we camped we were wet to the skin, hungry and tired, but not one word of grumbling could be heard. On May 14, 1863, we arrive at the outskirts of Jackson and meet the enemy. During the battle at Jackson a rather amusing incident happened. We were in line of battle and had moved up to the vicinity of a plantation around which were scattered a number of bee hives. Now, had we not been engaged with the enemy, our boys would have liked nothing better than to have despoiled those bees and supped on honey, but for the present we had important work on hand. The bees were quiet enough until the minie-balls went crashing through their hives, when they came out and rushed at us with terrible ferocity. Men can stand up and be shot at, all day, with the deadly musket, but when a swarm of bees pounces upon a company of men in concert, it's beyond human nature to stand it, and so two or three companies retired from the field. In fact, our lines were re-formed in that particular locality so as to avoid those Southern bees. They had no "rebel yell," but their charge on us was a successful one. We sometimes captured things we did not want. At Jackson we captured a smallpox hospital and its inmates. We didn't want it, you may be sure, for everybody kept at a respectful distance from it.

The battle of Jackson is fought, the final charge is made and the city is ours, Gen. Johnston and his army retreating to the north and east. The final charge made by the Iowa boys under Gen. Crocker of Iowa, was one of the most superb and gallant of the war. Gen. Grant said that, with the exception of Sherman and Sheridan, Gen. Crocker was the best division commander in the army. We are now 80 miles from Grand Gulf and 50 miles east of Vicksburg. Immediately the army is wheeled about and faced toward Vicksburg, and the march commences to that city.

CHAPTER IX.

On May 16, 1863, at Champion Hill, the enemy was encountered, strongly stationed, on a series of ridges or hills, naturally well adapted for defensive purposes. Here we met Gen. Pemberton's army of over 40,000 men coming out of the entrenched position in the city to make mince meat of Gran't army. The battle opened early in the forenoon and raged for half a day, in which only 15,000 soldiers, or a portion of Grant's army, was engaged. It was one of the hard-fought battles of the war and one of the most bloody. The battle was mainly fought by McPherson's 17th Army Corps and Hovey's division of the 13th Corps.

Gen. Logan's charge on the extreme right, about three o'clock in the afternoon, was one of the finest charges of troops that I witnessed during the war, and I was in nine different battles. It has been said that at the battle of

Champion Hill for a time there was as fierce fighting as any seen in the west. The colors of my regiment were riddled with bullets and our color guards were all killed or wounded. About three o'clock the enemy gave way and commenced a retreat towards Vicksburg.

After driving the enemy from the field those engaged all day were tired out and halted for a time on the battle field. I would like to portray the scene that we gazed upon. It was a horrible picture and one that I carry with me to this day. All around us lay the dead and dying, amid the groans and cries of the wounded. Our surgeons came up quickly and, taking possession of a farm house, converted it into a hospital, and we began to carry ours and the enemy's wounded to the surgeons. There they lay, the blue and the gray intermingled; the same rich, young American blood flowing out in little rivulets of crimson; each thinking he was in the right; the one conscious of it today, the other admitting now it were best the Union should be maintained one and inseparable. The surgeons made no preference as to which should be first treated; the blue and the gray took their turn before the surgeon's knife. What heroes some of those fellows were; with not a murmer or word; with no anaesthetic to sooth the agony, but gritting their teeth, they bore the pain of the knife and saw, while arms and legs were being severed from their bodies. There was just one case that was an exception to the rule. He was a fine-looking officer and Colonel of some Louisiana regiment of the Confederate army. He had been shot through the leg and was making a great ado about it. Dr. Kittoe, of our regiment, examined it and said it must be amputated; the poor fellow cried and howled: "Oh, I never can go home to my wife on one leg. Oh, oh, it must not be." "Well," said the gruff old surgeon, "that, or not go home at all." The Colonel finally said yes, and in a few minutes he was in a condition (if he got well) to wear a wooden leg when he went home to his wife.

The enemy are retreating to the city to get behind the breastworks, and Grant's army is pushing them right along every day. It is twenty days now since the campaign began. In that time the army has marched nearly 200 miles, beaten two armies in five different battles, captured 27 heavy cannon and 61 pieces of field artillery; taken 6,500 prisoners and killed and wounded at least 6,000 of the enemy. Starting without teams and with an average of three days' rations in the haversacks, we subsisted principally on forage found in the country. Only five days' rations had been issued in twenty days. Still, neither suffering nor complaint was witnessed in the command. The army was in fine condition, so Gen. Grant said. Since it had left Milliken's Bend it had marched by day and night, through mud and rain, without tents and on irregular rations. Gen. Grant said then: "My force is composed of hardy and disciplined men, who know no defeat and are not willing to learn what it is." Well, if marching day and night in the mud and rain, on short-rations, made us hardy, I reckon he told the truth. I tell you today, after 50 years have passed, I can remember the gnawing of hunger on that memorable march, and I recollect one day spying a piece of bacon rind at the road side, which some more fortunate soldier had thrown away, and grabbing it as a great treasure I removed the dirt and ate it with a ravenous appetite. Before we get to Vicksburg we must have another battle at the Big Black River. The enemy were discovered in force, strongly posted near the bridge. The day was hot and Gen. Lawler, who was rushing around in his shirt sleeves, discovered that by moving one portion of his brigade through the brush under cover of the river bank, the remainder to push directly against the left flank of the enemy, he could reach a position where he would be able to carry the works by storm. As soon as his troops were properly placed, Gen. Lawler led his boys in blue in a magnificent charge, capturing one entire brigade of the enemy, and forcing the remainder to beat a hasty retreat to Vicksburg.

On May 18, 1863, Gen. Grant's army invested the enemy's defenses of Vicksburg and then commenced a siege that lasted for 47 days, an account of which it is my purpose to give as concisely as possible. The enemy's breastworks encircled the city somewhat in the shape of a horseshoe, being about eight miles in length. The ground around the city is very rough; steep hills, deep gullies, underbrush, cane and willows and everything to impede the army. Gen. Grant, with about 30,000 men, had cooped up Gen. Pemberton and his army of over 35,000 men. (Seven weeks later P. surrendered 30,-

000 men.) Soon after Gen. Grant had assigned his several Corps Commanders to their places (Gen. Sherman being on the right, Gen. McPherson in the center and Gen. McClernand on the left), several charges were made at different points on the line, but owing to the strong forts and entrenchments, the enemy repulsed us with heavy loss. The union lines, however, are advanced, positions for artillery are selected, and the daily duel of the sharpshooters is opened up in the immediate front.

After so much marching and fighting, the boys in blue are weary and hungry, and a few days' rest is granted the men, that they may attend to some washing and cleaning up. Very few of us had a second shirt to wear. Toward the close of the war but few carried knapsacks; it wasn't necessary. It is related of an Irishman that, upon being asked why he didn't go to the Quartermaster and draw a knapsack, replied: "An' what do I want a knapsack for?" "Why, to put your clothes in, Pat." "Sure, an' if I should go on dress parade wid me clothes in me knapsack the Colonel would be after puttin' me in the guard house." May 21st we are furnished with a good square meal by Uncle Sam—if hard tack, sow bacon, beans and coffee can be called a square meal. We so considered it after the hardships of the last month. And having been strengthened in the inner man with plenty of food, Gen. Grant proposes to carry Vicksburg by storm on the morrow, May 22, 1863. Shall we ever forget that desperate charge? No, and I believe had Gen. Grant known at the time how strongly the enemy were entrenched and how valiantly they would fight, he would never have ordered that charge. He thought, no doubt, as we soldiers believed, that having been so successful in meeting the enemy recently, we could whip any armed force that opposed us. May 22, 1863, the order was given to commence the attack at

10 o'clock. At that hour the battle opened; every piece of artillery was brought to bear on the works; sharpshooters at the same time began their part; nothing could be heard but the continual shrieking of shells, the booming of cannon and the sharp whiz of the minie-ball. At the time the assault was attempted our bivouac was in a ravine just east of the "White House," or "Shirley House." Running in front of the house was the main Jackson wagon road leading into the city. For about five hundred yards the road had been cut down in the ridge to a depth of a man's head, then the ridge sloped a little and the road opened out in plain view of the forts of the enemy not 200 yards distant. We marched in columns of four through this cut in the road until we reached the point where we would be exposed to the enemy's guns, then we were to deploy to the left along the slope of the hill, until the entire regiment was out of the road, when at the word

of the commanding officer—"By the right flank, charge"—we were to go over the enemy's works. As we came out of that road Major Cowan gave the command, "double quick," and we started across that open space. Major Cowan, commanding the regiment, fell at the first volley from the enemy, having only taken a step or two.

The enemy was watching and the instant we appeared in sight they opened into us an awful volley of shot and shell. There was no one to give the command to halt, or right face and charge; the Major was killed and the ranking Captain didn't know it. We went as far in that hail of death as we thought would be sufficient for the regiment to form in line of battle, and then we dropped flat on the ground. Being First Sergeant of Company A of my regiment, I was at the head of the regiment with Major Cowan when we started across that deadly piece of open ground, the Major falling by my side, but I kept right on at the head of the regiment until space enough was given the regiment to form in line under the brow of the hill. The ground sloped down hill from the enemy's parapet, and by flattening one's self about as flat as a hard tack, he was comparatively safe from the musketry fire of the enemy. The regiment came through, but the dead and wounded lay thick over that stretch of 200 yards. The order to charge the works was, after a short time, given by the ranking Captain, and we started up the hill, to be met by a sweeping volley of musketry at short range, which mowed the men down in bunches. We could not return the fire, for the enemy were safe behind their breastworks. Some of our men reached the top of the parapet, but fell as fast as they climbed up. No troops could face such a destructive fire from a protected enemy. Presently the order is given to fall back, and we retire under the brow of the hill and remain there until after dark, when we took our usual place in the rear of the "White House." The charge of my regiment is but a picture of all other regiments that took part on that day. The assault was no more successful at other points of the line, and the Union army suffered great loss. The works were strongly constructed and well arranged to sweep the approaches in every direction; their position was too strong, both naturally and artificially, to be taken by storm. Wherever the assault was attempted, the hillsides were covered with the slain and wounded, many of them lying in the hot sun during the day crying for water, which could not be taken to them. Three thousand Union soldiers were killed or wounded in this disastrous charge; more men in this one charge were lost than were lost during the late Spanish War. The army was now made sadly sure that over ground so rough and with such strong forts and entrenchments it could not hope to carry Vicksburg by storm. It clearly proved the great advantage an army has in having breastworks and entrenchments to cope with the enemy. Gen. Grant had had such wonderful success so far that he really thought his troops could walk right up to and inside those fortifications. But the fact has been demonstrated that the loss of precious lives would be too great, and preparations for a siege were begun and the pick and shovel were brought into requisition. Saps and rifle trenches were constructed and in these our sharpshooters were continually on the lookout for the hidden enemy. Before we had constructed outer rifle pits so as to make them corparatively safe, our boys with their bayonets and a tin plate, dug little holes in the ground and on top of the earth placed a few fence rails. Between these rails our men could pick off the sharpshooters of the enemy and many a duel was had here between the pickets of the two armies.

CHAPTER X.

The duels between the sharpshooters of the two armies were fierce and deadly. All of us like heroes. There were many heroes beside the great Generals. Here is one from the ranks. John Battle Harrison was wounded at Shiloh and again at Champion Hills. When told by the surgeon to go to the hospital, he refused and remained fighting in the ranks with a wound that would have taken hundreds of others to the hospital. This brave soldier was killed in one of the sharpshooter duels. Our company was on duty on the skirmish line all day, and we could not bury him until night; then during the dark hours of the night we dug a grave on the hillside, and wrapping his blanket around him, we left him to sleep until the great reveille is sounded. I thought that night of the lines I used to speak in school when a boy:

> "Not a drum was heard, not a funeral note
>   As his corpse to the rampart we hurried;
> Not a soldier discharged his farewell shot
> O'er the grave where our hero we buried."

But we must not falter if our comrades do fall, but take up our duty of the soldier on the morrow and battle for the right. Now we are digging trenches and making breastworks, as well as running a sap toward the enemy's lines by using the sap-roller. My young friends may ask what a sap-roller is. We boys used to call it a "bullet-stopper." Suppose we take two empty barrels and lash them together, one on top of the other, then wrap them 'round and 'round with willow saplings, fill them with earth, put a cover on, lay them down, and you have a sap-roller. By keeping this in front of a couple of men, they could dig a trench directly toward the enemy's lines, and still be protected from the deadly minie-balls. We dug trenches and moved towards the enemy until the two picket lines were within hail of each other. One of the "Johnnies" made an agreement with one of our boys that they should lay down their guns and have a talk, which they did. The Confederate said our guns had killed many in the trenches. Sometimes there was a richness in the repartee between the Union and Confederate pickets that is worth repeating. One day a "Johnnie" calls out: "What are you men doing over there?" and quick comes the answer: "Guarding 30,000 Johnnies in Vicksburg, and making them board themselves." Another picket asks the question: "Why don't you come and take Vicksburg?" and the Union replies: "Oh, we're in no particular hurry; Gen. Grant is not yet ready to transfer you North." The pickets of both armies were good natured and used to brag of their ability to whip each other. The gunboats and mortars from the river side make things lively for the people inside the city. Day after day the sharpshooters are at work; the cannonading is kept up; the saps are approaching the enemy's stronghold still nearer and nearer. The bursting of shells over our heads, while resting in our camps, tended to make things lively, in many instances causing wounds and death. One day the boys of my regiment were cooking a mess of beans for dinner (beans were on the bill of fare every day). The beans were being cooked in one of those large camp kettles that were hung from a pole resting on two upright sticks driven into the ground. The beans were supposed to be done. The dinner hour was near at hand; two of the boys took hold of the pole and lifted the kettle from its resting place to put it to one side. Just then the sharp whirr of a piece of shell from overhead was heard and the next instant it went crashing through the bottom of that kettle, carrying beans and all with it, burying it in the earth. The two soldiers, still holding the pole in their hands, looked at each other in disgust for a moment, and then one of them, turning around, called out to the waiting hungry soldiers: "Boys, your beans have gone to h—l."

The boys in the ranks had no use for a "dude" officer. Gen. McPherson, who commanded our corps (a braver or finer gentleman never breathed), had on his staff a fine officer, but who was very fond of dress, and when he would ride along the line of march, in his velvet suit, the boys would guy him unmercifully. One day this Colonel came into the trenches, and, stopping opposite where I stood on the embankment behind the gabions, addressed one of our boys thus: "Sergeant, do you see the enemy from this point?" The Sergeant replied: "Yes, sir, by looking through this hole in the log, down that ravine you will occasionally see the enemy crossing." The Colonel got up, looked through the hole, and saw some Confederates crossing the ravine, and then he was moved to take a hand in the game, and turning 'round, said: "Sergeant, load your rifle and let me have a pop at those fellows." "All right, Colonel," and while he was still looking, the Sergeant at his rear, loaded the musket. The gun had been in use most of the day, and was pretty foul and if not held just right, would kick fearfully. Well, wicked sinner that the soldier was, he took two cartridges, using two charges of powder and one bullet, and loaded the Enfield rifle, put the percussion cap on and handed it to the Colonel and, stepping back into the trenches, awaited developments. The Colonel got ready, saw his man, pulled the trigger and—tumbled back into the trench. He handed the gun back, remarking: "Your gun, Sergeant, recoils considerable," and the innocent (?) soldier said, "Does it?" The Colonel did not ask for a second shot. I'll warrant he had a black and blue shoulder for a month. The poor Colonel has passed away and the Sergeant never had the opportunity to apologize to him.

The sap-roller with the boys in blue behind it are gaining every day in digging trenches toward Fort Hill. The men of Gen. Logan's division are employed in this work, and the plan is to undermine the enemy's Fort Hill and blow it up. While we had to be under fire from the enemy constantly, we were better off than they; not only did they suffer from a continuous shelling by the cannons and mortars, and the incessant rattle of musketry, but they had to do it on pretty empty stomachs, for toward the last they were reduced to a very meager diet, while we were having plenty of bacon, hard tack, coffee, etc. The price of food inside the city at that time was a little higher than in Chicago. How do these prices please you: Flour, $1,000 a barrel; meal, $140 a bushel; beef, $2.50 per pound, and mule meat, $1 per pound.

What could you expect when there was a

continuous siege of 47 days; a city surrounded by an army that neither permits any one to go into or come out of it; an army that slowly but surely is creeping up by its sap-rollers and approaches, getting closer and closer each day? I said we did not let any one into the city and none to come out of it; still, notwithstanding all our watchfulness there were a few who succeeded in getting through the lines, and a few that made the attempt but failed. Permit me to give one instance. In front of the line of the 15th Illinois Regiment, near the picket line, was a low marshy sink, of about an acre in size, covered by brush and dense cane brakes. One night a boy of about 10 years of age came out of the brush towards the picket line, holding up his handkerchief as a sign that he wished to surrender. The sentinel told him to come in; he did, and the little fellow told a pitiful story; that he had been in Vicksburg visiting his aunt who was sick; that his mother lived in Jackson, and he wanted to go home. The story seemed plausible and he was allowed to go through the lines. Not long after, one night, the pickets in that same locality, heard a rustling in the bushes in the same swampy hole, and surmising that something was wrong, surrounded it, demanding the surrender of any one there on pain of being shot at once. To their surprise out came a half-dozen men, each with a bag over his shoulder containing 10,000 percussion caps. Gen. Johnston had sent the men and caps back, led by the same little boy, and they were trying to get into Vicksburg. They were marched to Gen. Grant's headquarters, and while waiting to be ushered into the General's presence, one of the prisoners said to the boy: "What do you suppose they will do with you, for you are the fellow that got us into this fix?" The little fellow, cocking one eye in a comical manner, replied: "Oh, I guess they won't hurt me much, coz I'se so little." The little fellow was not hurt much, but kept a prisoner until the surrender and then with the soldiers sent home.

The siege continues day after day; the bombardment from land and water is incessant; the beleaguered army is reduced to quarter rations, living on mule meat and thinking it good fare; the inhabitants of the city hiding and living in caves, to escape the storm of shells from the Union army and navy, which are exploding day and night in their streets. The enemy are brave and fight valiantly for their city and cause; neither the scorching sun nor the drenching rain keep them from their posts. They suffer for water; they are pinched with hunger; still they fight and hold the fort. However, the end is near. That persistency and determination, so characteristic of our commander, Gen. Grant, will surely win. It is related of Gen. Grant that one day during the siege he was riding around the lines, and stopped at a house to get some water. The only occupant was a woman who tauntingly asked him if he expected to get into Vicksburg. "Certainly," he replied. "But when?" she said. "I cannot tell exactly when I shall take the town, but I mean to stay here till I do, if it takes me 30 years." The reply was too much for the old lady, and her heart sank within her, as she rushed back into the house to hide her anger. That reminds me of an incident that passed between Gen. Grant and myself, the relating of which I may be pardoned inasmuch as I am relating reminiscences. One hot day in June I was in the trenches with my company, behind the gabions, on duty as sharpshooters, when Gen. Grant, attended by one of his staff, came along. He had climbed the hill and when he arrived opposite me was perspiring and puffing greatly. We turned and saluted the General as he walked along the trench. When he came opposite to me he said: "Sergeant, is there any water convenient?" I replied, "None,

General, except what is in my canteen," and taking my canteen from my shoulder, half filled with pretty warm water, I handed it to him. He took it, offered it to the officer, who declined, and then Gen. Grant took a hearty drink from my canteen. He then handed it back, thanking me for it, and passed on. So in the words of Miles O'Reilly's poem—

"There are bonds of all sorts in this world of ours,
Fetters of friendship and ties of flowers,
And true lovers' knots, I ween;
The girl and the boy are bound by a kiss,
But there's never a bond, old friend, like this—
We have drank from the same canteen."

Although we are relieved often in our daily duty of sharpshooters, and return to the ravines and hollows where we are bivouacked, still we are constantly threatened with death; the soldiers wrote songs, and the jest went around, fun actually being coined from the danger which some comrade escaped, or attempted to nimbly dodge. There was no shirking or quailing; danger had long since ceased to cause any fear.

Exploding shells and whistling bullets attracted but little notice. Even death had become so familiar that the fall of a comrade was looked upon with almost stoical indifference; eliciting, perhaps, an expression of pity, and most generally the remark: "I wonder who will be the next one?" Men are not naturally unmindful of danger, nor do their hearts usually exhibit such indifference to human agony and suffering; yet the occurrence of daily scenes of horror and bloodshed, through which they passed, the shadow of the angel of death constantly hovering over them, made them undisturbed spectators of every occurrence, making the most of today, heedless of the morrow.

CHAPTER XI.

Let us go back to the "White House" and Fort Hill in our front. The Shirley or White House was not far from Fort Hill, and being on a hill overlooked much of the field of operations, and was the frequent resort of Gen. Grant and other commanders during the siege. Several officers and men were shot in this house. A Lieutenant of Battery L went to Colonel Maltby of the 45th Illinois (whose camp was along the "White House") and asked permission to use a room in the house for making out the battery pay rolls. "Why, certainly," promptly answered Colonel Maltby, "walk right in; it's a splendid place. I was shot in the leg here yesterday."

It is of peculiar interest to the writer, as he was wounded in this house while in the line of duty on July 2, 1863. Mr. Shirley and family were living in this house when on May 18, 1863, the skirmishers of the Union army advanced along the Jackson road, pressed back those of Pemberton's army into their main defensive line, so close at hand that the salient fort, known as Fort Hill to the Union army, but to the Confederates known as the Third Louisiana Redan, nearly west of the house and immediately north of the road, was not over 350 yards distant. As the building was an obstruction to the fire from the Confederate line, it was to have been destroyed; but, according to the story of Mrs. Eaton, the presence of her mother delayed carrying the order into execution so long that the Confederate soldier who came to do so, while holding a ball of blazing cotton to the building, fell under the fire of the advancing vanguard and was buried the next day upon the spot. As for Mrs. Shirley, she first had a sheet attached to a broomstick and hung from an upper window, which gave some respite from the fire of the Union troops. But their line soon reached the house itself and practically rested there, so that a steady firing upon it from the other side was inevitable. Notwithstanding this, Mrs. Shirley remained there for three days, much of the time sitting behind the large chimney for shelter. Having in the meantime learned of the situation of the Shirley's, orders came from Gen. McPherson for their removal. They went accordingly, into a shallow cave hastily prepared in a nearby ravine. Here the family remained for a time, Mrs. Shirley having sickened from exposure and poor fare, but were soon after, by Gen. Grant's personal direction, removed to a plantation three miles in the rear, where a negro cabin afforded temporary shelter. The Shirley's were Union people, and Mr. Lossing, the historian, says: "That the accomplished daughter kept a diary during the siege, each day's record closing with the prediction that success would crown the efforts of the Union army." The wish was father to the thought; her patriotism was rewarded with the heart and hand of the gallant Gen. Eaton of the United States army, and they were married about the close of the war. They now reside in Washington, and if the facts of their courtship and betrothal, conducted amidst the exciting scenes of a terrible siege, were known, it would no doubt be a very interesting romance. But what of the ladies who are in the besieged city? Many of them have left their fine mansions and taken up their abode in the holes and caves of the hills in and around the city, and so universal was this mode of living that the city in its desolation looked like a "prairie dog's village." One of the residents of the city afterwards said: "It got to be Sunday all the time; seven Sundays in the week to us anyway. We hadn't anything to do and the time hung heavy. Seven Sundays, and all of them broken up at one time or another in the day or in the night by a few hours of the awful storm of fire and thunder and iron and lead." The caves were sometimes fearfully crowded, always hot and close. Oftentimes a cave had from twenty to twenty-five people packed in it; no turning room for anybody, and the air so foul, sometimes, you could not have made a candle burn. A child was born in one of these caves one night during the siege. Generally, there is considerable noise around when a baby is born, but this fellow was welcomed with the booming of cannon and the fierce shriek of the screaming shell. I'll warrant, if he was like most boys, he tried to make all the noise he could. But he is no longer a baby, at least let us hope he is not, for he is old enough now to be a man all through, being at this time over 50 years of age. I have his picture and a fine-looking man he is. He writes on his picture: "I was born 12 feet under ground." One night a shell burst in front of one of these caves and stopped up the hole to such an extent the occupants came near smothering, and for a time there was some lively scratching of dirt for a breathing hole.

Fort Hill is said to be the key to Vicksburg. We have tried often to turn this key, and have as often failed—in fact, the lock is not an easy one, but we soon shall try the burglar's plan, and with the aid of powder blow the lock to "smithereens." The sap or trench is run to the fort and the fort is mined, the boys digging the dirt and carrying it out in boxes. Great holes are dug underneath the fort, and miners from the Lead Mine, 45th Illinois Regiment, who understand tamping, have charged the 2,200 pounds of powder, and all is ready to light the fuse. June, the 25th, a heavy artillery fire opened all along the line, and at 2:30 p. m., the explosion takes place. Huge masses of earth were thrown in the air, and the ground was shaken as by an earthquake. As soon as the earth was rent, a bright glare of fire issued from the burning powder, but quickly died away, as there was nothing combustible in the fort. A few Confederate soldiers were hurled into the air, one or two of whom came down inside our lines, and some were buried in the fort, as was proven a few years after the war, when the fort was dismantled and turned into a cotton field, a few skeletons were found buried underneath. One negro boy fell among the men of our company. He gathered himself together, and looked around as though he thought the day of judgment had surely come. One of our boys asked him how far up he thought he had gone, and he replied: "Don't know, Massa; 'bout free miles, I guess." He believed it, for I never saw such a frightened look on any one's face, and his eyes stood out and looked unnatural. When the smoke and dust had cleared away partly, a great saucer-shaped crater was seen, where before was the A-shaped Fort Hill. It was large enough to hold about 60 or 80 men. The 23rd

Indiana and the 45th Illinois were in the trenches ready to charge; the command was given before the dust had fully settled; the 23rd Indiana charging to the left of the crater to the top of the works; the 45th Illinois up and into the crater. The enemy had come up behind the big pile of earth thrown out by the explosion, and as we went into the crater, they met us with a terrible volley of musketry, but on the boys went, up and over the embankment with a cheer, the enemy falling back a few paces to an inner or second line of breastworks, where are placed cannon loaded with grape and canister, and these cannon belched forth their death-dealing missiles, in addition to the heavy musketry fire, with such telling effect that many of the brave boys fall to rise no more; the line wavers, staggers, and then falls back into the crater. The enemy charge on us, but we repel them at the west bank of the crater, and a hand-to-hand conflict rages for hours; hand grenades and

The 23rd Indiana and 45th Illinois Regiments charging Fort Hill after the explosion of the mine June 25th, 1863, at the siege of Vicksburg.

loaded shells are lighted and thrown over the parapet as you would play ball. These shells and hand grenades carry death, as many as a dozen men being killed and wounded at one explosion. It seems to me, in looking back, a wonder that anyone in that hot place was left to tell the story. I have witnessed our men grab these shells, at the risk of their exploding, and fling them back. Many a brave hero laid down his life in that death hole, or, as we most appropriately called it, "Fort Hell." The Chicago Tribune had its correspondent in the field and, in the issues of that paper on July 3 and 6, 1863, he speaks of the charge and fighting in the crater, saying: * * * "A wide embrasure in the embankment was made into which the noble Lead Mine Regiment, led by Colonel Maltby, rushed in and at once planted our banner amid a terrific fire from the enemy. The conduct of the 45th Illinois Regiment was grand in the extreme. Universal commendation is bestowed for the gallant manner that regiment performed the duty assigned it, and in no small degree upon the field officers who so nobly inspired the men by taking the advance and marching up to the muzzles of the enemy's guns, so near that for a time it was a hand-to-hand fight. The colors of the regiment planted on the parapet of the fort are literally torn to pieces by the shots of the enemy. Two of the field officers, Lieut. Col. Smith and Major Fisk, are no more. Col. Maltby is still suffering from a severe wound."

We fought at close range with the enemy over that embankment of earth, many of the men receiving bayonet wounds. A cypress log, with port holes cut on the under side, was brought into the crater, and in helping to place it on the parapet, Col. James A. Maltby was severely wounded by splinters from the log. A solid shot from a cannon hit the log, hurling it with terrific force against the Colonel and his small command. Gen. John A. Logan said of Col. Maltby, at the siege of Vicksburg: "He is the bravest man I ever saw on the field of battle." He was in the Mexican War, badly wounded at Chapultepec, then at Fort Donelson in 1862 and then at Vicksburg. He was justly promoted to be a Brigadier General for his bravery. A detail of about two companies would hold the crater for two hours or more, their rapid firing causing the rifles to become hot and foul, and the men weary and worn out, when two other companies would slip in and take their places. Badeau, in his history of Gen. Grant, says: "Details from Leggett's brigade relieved each other all night long, in their attempt to hold the crater." I want to correct his history and say, as I have a right to say, for I was there and speak from what I know to be the facts, it was no "attempt," it was an accomplished fact that we *held it*, but to our great loss, until the order was received to give it up. What a terrible sacrifice it was to hold that little piece of ground. It probably was all right to have made the charge into the crater after the explosion and try to make a breech inside the enemy's lines, but it surely was a serious mistake, either of Gen. Grant or Gen. McPherson, to cause that crater to be held for over 48 hours with the loss of brave men every hour. I remember, upon returning to the trenches, after having been relieved in the crater, of passing Gen. John A. Logan, surrounded by some of his aid-de-camp, and as they bore past him some wounded hero, he broke forth with vehemence, saying: "My God! they are killing my bravest men in that hole." Someone suggested that the place be given up. He said in reply: "I can't; my commanding officer orders me to hold every inch of ground." The crater was at last given up and we resumed the ordinary duties of everyday life in the trenches and in camp.

CHAPTER XII.

The army was without tents, yet very comfortable. They were encamped along the steep hillside, mostly sheltered from the enemy's shot. A place was dug against the hill, and in many cases, into it, forming a sort of cave. Poles were put up and covered with oil cloths, blankets or cane rods, of which an abundant supply was near at hand. For fuel, the farm fences were laid under contribution, in some cases being hauled for two or three miles. The work of slaughter and destruction went on day and night. The roar of cannon, the rattle of musketry, the sharp crack of the rifle in the hands of the sharpshooters, reached the ear from all sides. There was no cessation, no let up.

> "Cannon to right of them;
> Cannon to left of them;
> Cannon in front of them;
> Volleyed and thundered."

Stormed at with shot and shell, the beleaugered garrison and the inhabitants of Vicksburg must have felt, as surely as day follows night, that the end could not be much longer delayed. Mines and countermines were dug and sprung. Not a man in the trenches on either side could show his head above the breastworks without being picked off by the sharpshooters. A hat held out for two minutes at a port hole was riddled with minie-balls. Shells searched out all parts of the city, with direful results. Several women and children were killed and wounded during the siege. There were about 1,300 women and children in the city during the bombardment, who, during the greater part of the time, had been obliged to live in caves, cut in the hard clay hills in the city, of which there were several hundred. At this day it may seem to some of my readers that it was cruel and inhuman for the Union forces to fire on defenseless women and children, but what could we do; they were in the city and preferred to remain there to cheer on their husbands and brothers in their work of trying to destroy the Union. To show my readers with what feeling these Southern women showed their hatred of the North and the boys in blue, let me give a simple extract from a letter written by a Southern wife to her husband in the Confederate army, which letter was captured near Vicksburg. Speaking of the Yankees she says: "If there is an hereafter, a heaven or hell, I pray to go to perdition ere my soul would be joined to rest in heaven with the fiendish foe. It would be some solace to us, when we love our husbands, fathers, sons and friends, to know they were fighting an enemy, civilized or refined in a great degree. But, oh! the thought is killing; is too painful, to see our men, the choicest, most refined specimens of God's work, destroyed and even forced to take up arms against the offscourings, outcast dregs of creation, for every man they lose is a blessing, a Godsend to humanity and society." These are strong words, and a woman that could harbor such feelings would have the courage to stay in the doomed city and take her chances with her husband and friends.

To offset this, let me tell you of a romance of the war, which has never been published, and was given me by Comrade Searles, late of Chicago. Gen. Elias R. Dennis, in command of a brigade of our troops during the siege, made his headquarters at a farm house (the home of a widow and family), occupying one portion of it. The General was very kind to the widow and orphans, often providing for them from his own means. One of these children, a bright, winsome little girl of some eight years, took a deep interest in all that transpired, remembering many events of those stirring times, but above all, retaining a most kindly recollection of the General who occupied the house. About twelve years ago a reunion of some old veterans was held at Vicksburg. Comrade Searles, of

Chicago, was there, and among the Southern ladies who welcomed them was this little girl, now, of course, grown to womanhood. Accepting her kind invitation to visit her home, the next day found our comrade in the same house where Gen. Dennis had made his headquarters during the siege. Naturally, the conversation turned to the days of 1863. The lady, recalling the many kindnesses of Gen. Dennis, inquired if he were alive, to which Comrade Searles replied: "Why, bless you, I know him personally; he lives at Omaha." She then asked her comrade if he would be the bearer of a letter to the General, and he replied, "Most gladly." In due time this was delivered. What its contents were, none save the writer and the General ever knew, but as he read the letter, his lips quivered and his eyes filled with tears. The General was alone in the world, his wife and only daughter having passed away. Soon after he journeyed south. We know not what the greeting was; no doubt the lady awakened in the mind of the old veteran memories of his own lost, loved child, for shortly after this, he adopted the lady as his daughter. He lived the remainder of his days in Vicksburg, and but recently passed over to the eternal camping ground. When the General's will was proven, it was found that all his property had been left to his daughter of the Southland.

Another romance that commenced shortly after the surrender of the city is worth recording. A Miss Mary E. Hurlburt, of Danbury, Conn., a Northern girl, was visiting at the Lunn Mansion in the city of Vicksburg at the outbreak of the war, and tarrying too long, was compelled to remain there until the Union forces opened up the Mississippi River. When Gen. Grant captured the city, the officers of those commanding the troops in the city domiciled themselves at different houses. Gen. Leggett and his staff located their headquarters at the

Lunn residence. Gen. John A. Rawlins, chief of Gen. Grant's staff, had occasion to visit the headquarters of Gen. Leggett and naturally met Miss Hurlburt and their acquaintance soon ripened into a love affair, which in a few months culminated in a wedding and the young lady became the wife of Gen. John A. Rawlins, and shared with him in all the honors conferred upon the General as the closest advisor of Gen. Grant, and afterwards as Secretary of War.

The month of June, 1863, was rolling by and the glorious 4th of July drew near. The Union lines were getting closer and closer, and the question was passed around among the boys, "Shall we spend the Fourth in Vicksburg or in the trenches?" On June 28, the Confederates threw over to our men a small biscuit made of corn meal and peas. To this was attached a very small piece of meat and a note stating that it was one day's rations. The note went on: "We are pretty hungry and dreadful dry. Old

Pemberton has taken all the whisky for the hospitals and our Southern Confederacy is so small just now that we are not in the manufacturing business. Give our compliments to Gen. Grant and say to him that grub would be acceptable, but we will feel under particular obligations to him if he will send us a few bottles of good whisky."

Shall I give you the experience of a wounded soldier? Towards the close of the siege, while in the line of duty, a minie-ball from a Confederate sharpshooter went crashing through his right lung. His comrades bore him back a short distance; the surgeon came and seeing where the soldier had been shot, shook his head and said, "he cannot live." Comrades gathered around, saying in undertones, "poor fellow, he's got his discharge." The soldier closed his eyes, and although gasping for breath, as the warm life blood flowed from his wound and gushed from his mouth, saw something—his past life came before him like a living panorama; the good deeds and the evil of his life appeared in a few moments; he thought he was soon to be ushered into eternity, and how would it stand with him there. He breathed one little prayer: "O, Lord, spare my life and I will serve thee all my days." Presently the ambulance came and he was lifted tenderly into it, to be conveyed two miles to the rear to the brush hospital. The boys said "good bye." He was but a youth, not twenty years of age; had been promoted to First Sergeant after the battle of Shiloh and had endeared himself to all in his company, many of whom were old enough to be his father. Louis LaBrush, a Sergeant of the company, a Frenchman by birth, but a true lover of his adopted country, loved this smooth-faced boy, so badly wounded, and begged permission of the Captain to go with the wounded soldier and watch over him. The Captain, seeing the yearning look in the eyes of the Sergeant, granted permission, and the ambulance started with the old Sergeant watching with a tender care over the little Orderly Sergeant pillowed on his knee. The sun was just sinking to rest when they reached the hospital, which was only a brush shed covered with branches from the trees, in which were long lines of cots upon which the wounded soldiers lay. As the ambulance drew near the surgeon in charge came out, and looking at the wounded man, said: "Put him out there under that tree; he'll die tonight," and the old Sergeant put his darling boy out under the tree, laying him tenderly on the ground. The Sergeant and another comrade of his company, Henry Winter, who was a nurse in the hospital, watched by the boy's side during the weary hours of the night. At midnight, as the doctor was making his rounds, he observed the Sergeant still under the tree, and went to see if the boy was yet living. Finding that he was, he then made an examination by probing with his fingers into the wounds. The splintered bones pierced the tender flesh and made the boy writhe in pain, although the only protest was the gritting of his teeth. To cause his boy such suffering, after the treatment he had received, was more than the old Frenchman could stand, and he burst forth in a volley of oaths, commanding the doctor to take his hands off immediately or he would kill him, saying, "If he is going to die, let him die in peace; you shall not kill him." Seeing the fire in the old Sergeant's eyes, the doctor went away, muttering, "Well, the boy will die anyway." I want to say right here, that as a rule our surgeons were men of sympathy and did all they could for the soldiers. The example I speak of is one of the exceptions. The next morning the surgeon did not come, but sent word that if the soldier under the tree was still alive, to dress his wound, give him clean clothing and place him on a cot in the hospital. He was alive and that boy recovered, even after the surgeon in the army and the doctors at home said he couldn't live. That wounded boy lives today and is able to write this book in the year 1915, and he is ever grateful in remembrance of the old French Sergeant and Comrade Henry Winter, whose tender care aided in saving his life.

CHAPTER XIII.

The trite saying of Gen. Sherman that "war is hell" cannot be fully appreciated by the people of this generation; only those who have been through the horrors of war on the battle field and in the hospitals, can fully realize the horrors of war. Let me tell you how one brave man of my company lost his life through the most reckless foolishness. One day during the siege he succeeded in procuring some whisky from some unknown source and drank enough of it to make him half drunk. While in this condition he took it into his head to go out in the open and march out towards Fort Hill, and finding something of interest in the open field, he brought it to camp and boasted to the boys where he got it. Some one went and reported to the First Sergeant that E——— was drunk and had said that he was going to walk right up on top of Fort Hill. The Sergeant detailed a Corporal to watch E——— and keep him in camp, but the soldier having enough whisky in him to make him reckless and without reason or sense, escaped his watch and went boldly up to Fort Hill and climbed the fort, but when on top a bullet from the enemy laid him low. As we boys got the body of our comrade that night and buried it, we could not help but say, that if poor E——— had let the accursed whisky alone he would have been living, and we then declared that liquor was a greater enemy than the men who opposed us with their muskets.

On the 3rd day of July, 1863, a white flag was seen, nearly opposite to the "White House." Firing ceased in that vicinity and presently several Confederate officers approached our lines to confer with Gen. Grant. The General declined meeting them, but sent word he would meet Gen. Pemberton at 3 o'clock in front of Gen. McPherson's lines. Soon after Gen. Pemberton came out and met Gen. Grant under a big tree, about midway between the two lines, where they had a conference as to the surrender of Vicksburg, "The Gibralter of America." After a talk of an hour, possibly, Gen. Pemberton returned inside the fortifications, and then after correspondence lasting until the next day, terms of surrender were finally agreed upon, and on Saturday, July 4, 1863, the anniversary of American Independence, the garrison of Vicksburg marched out of the works it had defended so long, and stacking their arms, hung their colors on the center, laid off their knapsacks, belts and cartridge boxes, and thus shorn of the accoutrements of the soldier, marched down the road into the city. They went through the ceremony with that downcast look, so touching on a soldier's face. Not a word was spoken, save the few words of command necessary to be given by their officers, and these were given in a subdued manner. What an army it was—30,000 men and 172 cannon. Gen.

J. B. McPherson, commanding the 17th Army Corps, addressed a letter to Col. Rawlins, chief of staff to Gen. Grant, saying, "If one regiment goes in advance to the court house to take possession, I respectfully request that it be the 45th Illinois. This regiment has borne the brunt of the battle oftener than any other in my command and always nobly." Col. Rawlins endorsed this letter, stating that it was left to Gen. McPherson to designate such regiment as he saw proper to go forward and take possession of the court house. Gen. McPherson then sent a letter to Gen. John A. Logan, commanding the third division: "I suggest that the 45th Illinois take the advance in going into the city." Now the boys in blue take up their line of march into the city. Gen. Badeau, in his history of Gen. Grant says: "Logan's division was one of those which had approached nearest the works, and now was the first to enter the town. It had been heavily engaged in both assaults and was fairly entitled to this honor. The 45th Illinois Infantry marched at the head of the line and placed its battle-torn flag on the court house in Vicksburg. Gen. Grant and Gen. Logan rode into the town at the head of Logan's division."

When inside the works, and in the city, the men of the two armies affiliated at once. Groups of Union and Confederate soldiers could be seen wherever there was a shady place; the Union soldier pumping the rebel and giving him in return for the information hard tack and bacon, which the poor famished fellows accepted with a grateful look. The Confederates reclined on the grass and while munching their hard tack, tell what they "reckon" is their loss; how long they "allowed" to hold out; how our sharpshooters killed "right smart" of their men and they wish "we'uns" and "you'uns" could have this war ended and all live together in peace. Many of the Union and Confederate soldiers were seen walking arm in arm; they felt they were countrymen. Five days' rations were issued to the prisoners, consisting of bacon, hominy, peas, coffee, sugar, soap, salt and crackers.

Here is what one of the Confederates wrote about it: "How the famished troops enjoyed such bounteous supplies, it is needless to state. For once the brave boys were now objects of their enemy's charity. They grew jovial and hilarious over the change in their condition. The Yankees came freely among them and were unusually kind. They asked innumerable quesaions and were horrified at the fact of the men eating mules and rats." After feeding and paroling this large army of men, for it took several days to parole them, they silently and sadly marched out and off to their homes, while the boys in blue and the people of the North were full of rejoicing. Here is a few lines, composed by one of the boys in blue at the time:

"The armies of the Union
'Round Vicksburg long had lain,
For forty-seven days and nights,
Besieging it in vain.
Then came the morning of the Fourth,
Our nation's jubilee.
Ah, could the news this hour go forth,
In Vicksburg soon we'll be.
The siege is done, the struggle past,
On this eventful day;
Glad tidings crown us as at last
Our thanks to God we pay."

Yes, Old Glory floated over Vicksburg on July 4, 1863, and what rejoicing there was throughout the North when the news came to your homes that Vicksburg had fallen. Yes, Old Glory still floats there, and may we earnestly hope it will continue to wave as long as the city remains. We can rejoice today that we live to see a reunited people with one country and one flag. But while rejoicing, let us not forget those who have died on fields of honor, and while the years glide on, let the dead of Raymond, Champion Hills and Vicksburg never be forgotten. Let us think of them as standing guard over our dearly won prize, until the bugle sounds for silence, while the angel calls the roll. The third largest national cemetery in the United States is located at Vicksburg. Each of the small head stones marks the resting place of a hero. Seventeen thousand Union soldiers are buried in the 50 acres in this consecrated spot, of which 12,957 have the simple inscription, "Unknown," marked on their head stones. But they are not unknown to Him who cares for all. He takes cognizance of the heroes who fell fighting for their country and for freedom. Although their names are missing from the roster of the city where their ashes lie, still the great Jehovah keeps the record of the brave, and He will reward them in His own good time.

CHAPTER XIV.

At the request of Captain W. T. Rigby, Chairman of the National Military Park Commission of Vicksburg, to visit that place for the purpose of locating the positions held by my regiment during the siege in 1863, I did visit Vicksburg, Miss., in August, 1902.

I found the weather very hot, 99 degrees in the shade. However, it was not as hot as it was when we were in that "crater" at Fort Hill, years ago. The people of Vicksburg greeted me with a glad hand. The contrast of long ago was striking. About the first man I met was an old grizzled veteran wearing the Confederate button and, seeing my G. A. R. button, he came up, and, extending his hand, greeted me: "How are you, comrade; we wear different buttons, but we are brothers;" and I shook his hand heartily and we had a pleasant chat of the siege. Then, we were shooting minie-balls at each other; now, our shots were story and laughter.

Captain Rigby drove me out to the Federal and Confederate lines. Many changes have taken place. Some few of the trenches and breastworks remain, but many have been smoothed off for the plow. As we drove to the spot where we camped, near the old "Shirley House," I said to myself, "Am I dreaming?" Can it be that this quiet, deserted place, overgrown with weeds and bushes, with no sound save the sweet songs of the birds in the trees is the same spot where, in the summer of 1863, so much life and action was seen each day; and where, instead of the music of the birds, it was the music of the whizzing minie-ball or the shrieking shell. In thought I went back to those days of noise and blood, and I involuntarily looked over to Fort Hill to see if the Confederate stronghold was still there, and listened to hear the sharp crack of the sharpshooter's rifle from the trenches, but all is quiet and hushed. I am soothed by the stillness, the quiet and peace that pervades these hills and ravines, and I wander in memory's hall of the long ago, when I am brought back to the present by Captain Rigby, with: "Now, Crummer, you must locate the position of the camp of your regiment during the siege." This I proceeded to do, having no difficulty, for the "Shirley House" is still there, although tumbling down and going to ruin. Thanks to the Illinois Commission, headed by Gen. John C. Black and others, Congress has made an appropriation to have the "Shirley House" restored to its former state. This house will be remembered for its prominence during the siege as a place of observation by general officers and as headquarters of the 45th Illinois. Quite a number of officers and soldiers were shot in this house by the Confederate sharpshooters.

I wandered through its ruins and you cannot imagine my feelings as I stepped into the northwest room and stood on the identical spot where on July 2, 1863, in the afternoon, while writing out an ordinance report, a Confederate sharpshooter sent a minie-ball through my right lung.

I placed marker 403 as the center of our camp and No. 484 marks the right of the camp of the 45th Regiment. This done, we approached Fort Hill on the Jackson road, and although the intrenchments and forts have been generally leveled off for agricultural purposes, changing the face of the hills, yet there is enough left to show where the main lines were. No. 489 marks the point where Major L. H. Cowen, 45th Illinois, was killed in the assault on the afternoon of May 22, 1863. The charge was made by the regiment, by right, in front. Major Cowen and myself were in the lead and running together when he fell. Being Orderly Sergeant of Co. A, it was my duty to be there.

No. 488 marks the center of the line of the 45th Illinois at the time of its closest approach to the Confederate line in the assault of May 22, 1863.

While walking over this ground I remembered how close we hugged that sloping hill, lying there in the scorching sun, with no chance to return the withering fire of the enemy.

Captain Rigby then asked me if I could locate the "crater" and Gen. Logan's line of approach to it. I walked over the hill, groping my way through the tall weeds and undergrowth, and, coming back to the captain, reported, by saying, "I can." "Good," he said; "you may drive the markers." I then drove marker No. 487 at the center of the west line of the crater made by the explosion under the 3rd Louisiana Redan (we called it Fort Hill) June 25, 1863. It may be questioned why I could be so certain about the location of the "crater," in as much as the fort had been completely demolished. My principal reason is this: Sergeant Esping, of our regiment, who fell in the "crater," pierced by a ball through his brain, was by my side at the time. We were together in the northwest corner of the "crater" and we had a splendid chance of doing good work, by looking off down the ridge to the right and northwest from the "crater," and firing on the Confederates in the trenches. Those old trenches where the Confederates were on June 25, 1863, are still there, so in walking over the hill and getting the right angle to those trenches, I was able to locate the "crater."

Markers Nos. 485 and 486 indicate the line of Logan's sap, or approach, to Fort Hill, commencing at the Jackson road. Captain Rigby thanked me heartily for my services of the day.

The 45th Illinois Infantry bore an honorable part in the siege, as the official records show.

The report of our Brigade Commander, Gen. M. B. Leggett, published in the official records at Washington, under date of July 6, 1863, relative to the charge and fighting in the "crater," is interesting and tends to corroborate the writer's statements.

* * * "At 3:30 p. m. of June 25, 1863, my command was in readiness, the 45th Illinois being the first, supported by the other regiments of the brigade and Lieut. H. C. Foster of the 23rd Indiana, with 100 men, being placed in the left hand sap, with orders to charge with the 45th Illinois, provided they attempted to cross the enemy's works. At 4:30 o'clock the mine was sprung and before the dirt and smoke was cleared away the 45th Illinois had filled the gap made by the explosion and were pouring deadly volleys into the enemy. As soon as possible loop-hole timber was placed upon the works for the sharpshooters, but the enemy opened a piece of artillery at very close range on that point and the splintering timbers killed and wounded more men than did balls, and I ordered the timbers to be removed. Hand grenades were then freely used by the enemy, which made sad havoc amongst my men, for, being in the crater of the exploded mine, the sides of which were covered by the men, scarcely a grenade was thrown without doing damage, and in most instances horribly mangling those they happened to strike. The 45th Illinois, after holding the position and fighting desperately until their guns were too hot for further use, were relieved by the 20th Illinois. The 20th Illinois was relieved by the 31st Illinois and they in turn by the 56th Illinois, but, their ammunition being bad, they were unable to hold the position and were relieved by the 23rd Indiana; the 17th Iowa then relieving the 23rd Indiana, and the 31st Illinois relieving them, held the position until daylight,

when the 45th Illinois relieved them and held the position until 10:00 a. m. of the 26th; the 124th Illinois then relieved the 45th Illinois and held the position until 5:00 p.m., when I received orders to withdraw to the left hand gap, where I maintained the position until the surrender on July 4th, when, by order of Major General Logan, my brigade led by the 45th Illinois, was honored with the privilege of being the first to enter the garrison, and the flag of the 45th Illinois the first to float over the conquered city."

The National Park Commission are doing a noble work. Capt. Rigby is the right man in the right place and with a corps of engineers is working day and night to make a beautiful park for the delight of the people that come after us. The state of Iowa has done the noble thing in appropriating $150,000 to place monuments in the park on the spot which the different Iowa regiments occupied during the siege. The Illinois legislature has also made an appropriation of $250,000 for monuments for the 78 different organizations engaged in that memorable siege. When the memorial tablets from the different states shall have been placed and the park fully laid out and completed, it will be one of the notable historic battle fields of the Union, and one which we of the North will occasionally visit with great interest. And now I close my sketch with this prayer: that war may never come to our fair land again, but that blessed peace, prosperity and righteousness may ever be our heritage.

GENERAL U. S. GRANT

From a photograph taken in Galena, Illinois, at the close of the Civil War.

GENERAL U. S. GRANT

CHAPTER XV.

AN APPRECIATION.

My closing chapter will be about our great commander, General Ulysses S. Grant, giving a few personal incidents of his life.

Orators, authors and statesmen have spoken and written of the great General so much it would seem as though there was nothing more could be said. However, as one who followed him through numerous battles during the Civil War, and who, at the close of the war, became a resident of Galena, Ill., and became personally acquainted with, and attended the same church as the General, I feel I have the right to note down, before the bugle sounds taps, a few words of appreciation of the man I knew.

For four years, just after the close of the war, I was in the employ of Col. W. R. Rowley, who was then Clerk of the Circuit Court of Jo Daviess County, Ill., and who had been one of the close family staff of General Grant during the early part of the war.

General John A. Rawlins and Colonel Rowley were neighbors of the General before the war and knew him well and intimately, and it is believed by the citizens of Galena, and known by many prominent men in the army, that these two men had more to do in helping and advising General Grant during the early part of the war, and, indeed, all through the war, so far as General Rawlins is concerned, than any of his Generals or friends in Congress or out of it.

Colonel Rowley and myself naturally had many conversations over the incidents of certain battles and about General Grant.

During the war and after, the enemies of Grant circulated many stories about his being drunk on this and that occasion.

If I wanted to stir Colonel Rowley up to a

fighting mood, and hear him use a "big, big D" (for he could use them occasionally), I would ask him: "Colonel, how about this new yarn of Grant's being drunk at Shiloh when the battle commenced?" The question was the spark that exploded the magazine of wrath and the Colonel would reply: "All a d—d lie. Wasn't I there with him all the time; don't I know. When will all the d—d liars get through telling their d—d lies about Grant." And then I would chuckle to myself and say: "Them's my sentiments, too."

It has been said of General John A. Rawlins (chief of General Grant's staff), and, I believe, it must be true, for Colonel Rowley once told me it was; that when Rawlins got mad he could use more "cuss words" than any man in the army. General Grant never used "cuss words," but he loved these two men, notwithstanding their habit of emphasizing their remarks sometimes with a big D.

Grant loved his friends and was always true to them. Grant wouldn't lie; even in small matters he insisted that the truth should be spoken. It is related of him that, after he became President and while one day he was busy with his cabinet, some one called to see the President. One of the cabinet officers directed the servant to say to the caller that the President was not in. "No," said the General; "tell him no such thing. I don't lie myself and I don't want my servants to lie for me."

A great man who was associated with him in public life has said of him: "He was the most absolutely truthful man I ever met in all my experiences." Another man who knew him well said of General Grant: "He hated two classes of men—liars and cowards."

General Grant never aspired to political office, although urged by his friends to do so. Just after the fall of Vicksburg some of the leading citizens of Galena visited him at that place. One day, in a general conversation, one of them asked what office he would like to have after the war was over. He replied that there was one office he would like to have when he returned to Galena. His friends pledged him their best endeavors in aiding him for whatever he might seek, and, being pressed to name the office, Grant said: "I would like to be alderman from my ward long enough to have a sidewalk built to my residence." Of course, there was a laugh and the matter was dropped. Upon his first visit to his old home at Galena, at the close of the war, the little city of many hills got up a reception upon a grand scale for its hero. The city was smothered with flags and decorations; the streets arched with flags and words of welcome. When the General arrived amid the booming of cannon and the huzzas of the people, he was hurriedly lifted into a barouche and started up the street at the head of a long procession. The first arch he met had in large letters: "General, the sidewalk is built." The General laughed and remarked: "I see my friends remembered I wanted to be alderman."

After his first nomination for the Presidency he was with us at Galena during the campaign, and had you seen the General moving around so quietly and unostentatiously among his neighbors and friends, you would have wondered that it could be the man who had just been declared the greatest military hero of the age, and that he was soon to be at the head of the nation.

His record as President for eight years, and the honored guest of all nations during his tour around the world, is an open history to all.

Upon his return from his trip 'round the world, the General and family took up their abode in Galena. The city again welcomed its hero to his old home amid the plaudits of thousands that came from near and far to tread its stony streets and pay their tribute of respect and honor to the modest, silent man known the world over. I think the General was more stirred to the heart with the kind tokens of love and friendship and honor which his old neighbors and citizens of Galena showered upon him than he was from all the attentions of nobility the world 'round.

General Grant's home life and his life among the people of Galena, even after the world had acclaimed him the greatest General of the ages, and honors had been showered upon him by the crowned heads of the world, was that of a quiet, unobtrusive, simple life like his neighbors and citizens.

We loved him as a neighbor and citizen. We said among ourselves: "Grant's head is the same size it was before the war."

He has been called the "silent man." Yes, he was rather guarded in his talks among men generally, but I want to say (for I have listened to him), that when among his friends and neighbors, if you could get him started, he was one of the most entertaining talkers I ever listened to.

During the month of June, 1880, while the Republican Convention was in session in Chicago, General Grant and family were living in Galena. He had held the Presidency two terms; he had also been 'round the world, feted and honored everywhere by kings and emperors, and now he had returned to the hills of old Galena to spend his days in rest and quiet; but his friends, who believed in him, urged him to again stand for the nomination for the Presidency. His friends of Galena, Ill., knew what his personal wishes were; he did not wish to again resume the burdens of office. However, according to the request of his family, especially his wife, and also to his political friends, he finally consented to make the run. You will remember what a fight there was in the convention—how the immortal 300, led by Roscoe Conkling, clung to the silent hero to the last.

While the Convention was in progress, each day the General came down town about 10 o'clock and spent an hour or two with his old friend and comrade, Colonel W. R. Rowley. Rowley was then Judge of the County Court, and I was clerk of the same court. Some of the friends were privileged to be there. I remember distinctly that all of us were intensely interested in every telegram that came to the office, but the General paid very little attention to them. He kept us entertained with most vivid recitals of what he had seen and heard in his travels 'round the world.

There was one man's name before the Convention who had a few votes as nominee for President. This man had been a trusted friend of General Grant in former years, but his actions had caused many of the General's friends to doubt his friendship. One afternoon, while we were in General Rowley's office, a telegram came that convinced Rowley and the friends that this man, while pretending undying friendship for the General, was playing him false. Rowley and others were outspoken in their denunciation of the course of this man who had helped Grant in former years and who Grant had helped so much in the past. The General was as calm and placid as though everything was lovely, his only remark being: "He was my friend when I needed friends, if I can't trust him, I can't trust anybody." The friend referred to was Hon. E. B. Washburne.

Hon. Roscoe Conkling said of General Grant: "Standing on the highest eminence of human distinction, modest, firm, self poised, having filled all lands with his renown, he has seen not only the high born and the titled, but the poor and lowly in the uttermost parts of the earth rise and uncover before him. The name of Grant shall glitter a bright and imperishable star in the diadem of the Republic when those who have tried to tarnish it are moldering in forgotten graves and when their names and epitaphs have tarnished utterly.''

This is a noble tribute of one great man for another; but we, his humble neighbors of Galena, Ill., who knew the General so well, love to think of the home life of this great man. One characteristic of his life is not generally known, and I make bold to set it down in type that all the world may know it. General Grant was a lover of his wife all through his married life. A little secret of the home life of this devoted man was known among the women of Galena, for they would tell their husbands what a lover General Grant was, and to prove it they would tell us that the General laced his wife's shoes for her.

While General Grant and Mrs. Grant were in Europe they paid a visit to the tomb of Ferdinand and Isabella. The thought of the ashes of the royal couple sleeping side by side through the centuries appealed to the devoted husband, and, turning to his wife, he said: "Julia, that is the way we should lie in death." So, when the Great General died they found a memorandum left by him as to his last resting place. First, he preferred West Point above others, but for the fact that his wife could not be placed beside him there. Second, Galena, or some place in Illinois. Third, New York; hence it is that in the beautiful tomb at Riverside, the resting place of the General, there is room for the ashes of Mrs. Grant.

After General U. S. Grant had answered the last roll call at Mount McGregor, in 1885, and the sad news came to his friends and neighbors of his former home, among the hills of the quaint old city of Galena, Ill., preparations were made to have a memorial service in the Methodist Church, where he had worshiped before and after the war. The church was draped in mourning. In front of the pulpit was a stand of pure white flowers, with the intials, U. S. G., in purple flowers.

The pew formerly occupied by the General when here was covered with the United States flag, tastefully draped. The house was filled with his friends and neighbors, and a feeling of personal loss was felt by all. The services were simple but beautiful. Several of his personal friends spoke feelingly of the Great General's life, among them the writer, and I am persuaded to close this appreciation by quoting my tribute given in 1885, in Galena, upon that occasion:

"The years glide swiftly by, the gray hairs come creeping on, and we boys of the army of twenty years ago are no longer boys, but men, whose numbers lessen each day as the months roll by.

Twenty-four years have passed since we donned the blue and marched down the streets and off to war. The forms and faces and events of those times at this distance seem unreal and shadowy, like the remembrance of a dream, and yet today, in the midst of the great sorrow that hangs over the land over the fall of our great cheiftain, we are again reminded of the waving flags and fluttering scarfs, the inspiring strains of martial music, the shrill notes of fife and drum, and the booming of cannon. We are today again reminded (for the death of our hero brings to us vividly the past days in which he took so great a part). I say, again are we reminded of the tears and prayers and promises—the music of soft voices and gentle words, the brave words spoken by mothers, sisters, sweethearts, the parting words, the last goodbye. We cannot forget, nay, we live over again the battles of Donelson, Shiloh, Corinth, Vicksburg and other victorious battlefields following our hero, whose memory we are tonight to cherish and revere.

"All these dear and sacred memories of those stirring times come wafted to us today like the weird airs of an Æolian harp swept by unknown winds, and the ear is touched, and through the brain, nerve and soul, and our hearts beat in sympathy and unison.

"So, tonight, as a nation mourns the fall of the Great Commander, we boys of the twenty-four years ago are more than privileged to add our tears of sorrow as we follow in spirit our hero to his last resting place.

"We boys loved him. Often he led us amidst the storm of shot and shell and where death faced us on every hand; but we soon learned that although it meant hard fighting to follow General Grant, yet it always promised victory, and that gave us inspiration to fight harder.

"General Grant was a man of transcendent military ability. In the book of fate it was written: 'He shall be a chief and a captain.' But above all he was a manly and a pure man.

He was tender and trusty and true.

"'The bravest are the tenderest,
The loving are the daring.'

"I always admired the humble side of his character. I think humility was one of his finest traits; although feted and honored as no man of this continent ever has been, he never for a moment showed any signs of realizing his greatness, or evincing a desire to count the honors conferred. Retiring in disposition, yet bold and brave to act when necessity demanded it, I speak of him in loving memory. You all knew him here in his former home, and who with him have worshiped oftimes in this church, and you all know that he was the bravest of the brave and the truest of the true.

"'His mein, his speech, were sweetly simple;
But when the matter matched his mighty mind,
Up rose the hero; on his piercing eye

Sat observation; on each glance of thought,
Decision followed.'

"As the day came, so duty appeared, and the brave old General took it up and did it earnestly and well.

"How well great battles and campaigns were planned and fought; how safely and wisely he guided the ship of state; how modestly he received honors of the world from crowned heads; how gladly he returned to the walks of a humble citizen; how bravely and patiently he suffered through his terrible affliction—are they not all known to us, and are they not written upon the pages of history for our children's children to read and study?

"Is it weak, that we who followed the ever-victorious flag of our great Commander, and who with him stood in trying places against evil and treason, should drop our tears upon the fallen form of him whom we loved? Nay, but let them fall, they but speak in louder tones than words can, of the love and regard we had for him, who, as the years roll by, will be honored and extolled as one of the greatest of all nations.

"Around the throne of the Eternal God must hover the spirit of such as he who lived without ever having a selfish thought.

"The steadfast friend, the gallant soldier, the great Commander has fallen asleep.

"Rest thee, friend, soldier, patriot,
Thy work is done."